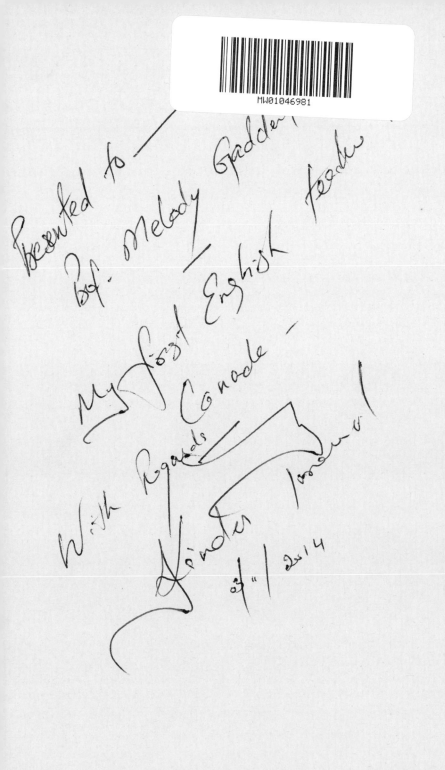

Presented to —
Prof. Melody Gadde[r]

My first English
teacher
Canada —

With Regards

[signature]
27/7/2014

TANDOORI DEMOCRACY

TANDOORI DEMOCRACY

Campaign 2012 for Punjab Assembly

Dr. Shinder Purewal

ISBN : 978-81-212-1213-7

Price: ₹ 525

First Published 2014

Published by

Gyan Publishing House
23, Main Ansari Road, Daryaganj,
New Delhi - 110002
Phones : 23282060, 23261060
Fax : (011) 23285914
E-mail: books@gyanbooks.com
website: gyanbooks.com

Laser Typesetting : PrePSol Enterprises Pvt. Ltd.
Printed at : G. Print Process Delhi

Cataloging in Publication Data--DK
  Courtesy: D.K. Agencies (P) Ltd. <docinfo@dkagencies.com>

Purewal, Shinder.
    Tandoori democracy : campaign 2012 for Punjab Assembly / Shinder Purewal.
      p.   cm.
    Includes bibliographical references (p.   ).
    ISBN 9788121212137

    1. Punjab (India). Legislature. Legislative Assembly--Elections, 2012. 2. Political campaigns--India--Punjab. 3. Political crimes and offenses--India--Punjab. I. Title.

DDC 324.70954552   23

Dedication

For my mother, Sardarni Darshan Kaur,
and in the memory of my father,
Late Sardar Gurdev Singh.

Contents

Foreword

One-third of India's law makers, both at state and national levels, have criminal cases pending against them. These criminal cases include rape, murder, attempted murder, kidnapping, robberies, extortion etc. This book locates the challenge of criminalization of politics in the electoral politics of India.

The flourishing role of money in campaigns has increased the dependence of political parties on the criminal elements of society. The growing use of drugs, alcohol and cash to woo the voters has paved the way for unsavory elements of society to expand their hold on the domain of politics.

Tandoori Democracy narrates the story of this process of criminalization of politics by objectively depicting campaign 2012 for Punjab Vidhan Sabha. The book is written with an objective to enlighten all Indians about the challenges of criminal elements to our democratic institutions. Times are calling for electoral reforms to save our democracy.

Preface

The basic premise of liberal democracy is that humans are born free, and equal in dignity and rights. Humans can enjoy these freedoms only with a constitutional framework guaranteeing basic human rights, such as the right to vote, the right to be a candidate, freedom of association, freedom of press, freedom of speech etc. The foundation of such freedoms and liberties must be based on the rule of law. At the government level, this means the separation of powers and checks and balances entrenched in the constitutional framework. On the level of society, it involves the concept of legal culpability where people enjoy freedom from arrest. One should be arrested only for breaking a law, not on the basis of any arbitrary whims of those in power. It also means the law must apply equally to all, even to those who exercise authority in the state. Everyone must be equal before the law, and the law applies to all in an impartial fashion. Above all, a democracy cannot survive without a separate and independent judiciary. The fathers of Indian Republic gave such a system to India, which has survived to date against all odds.

Democracy also teach us that free and fair democratic elections are necessary to establish legitimate authority. It is this electoral process that has presented an internal challenge to democracies everywhere. The challenge comes from the increasing role of money in campaigns. The recently concluded Congressional and Presidential elections cost more than 6 billion dollars to candidates and parties. Both Presidential candidates, Mitt Romney and Barak Obama, collected and spent more than 2 billion dollars on their campaigns. There had been serious allegations against the former French President Sarkozy for taking millions from Colonel Qaddafi for his campaign. When a lone demonstrator stood against a column of tanks in Beijing's Tiananmen Square during the 1989 student uprising, he was inspired by the ideals of the American constitution. He and his fellow demonstrators were attracted to the concepts of 'life, liberty and the pursuit of happiness' and the rule of law. From Tiananmen Square to Tahir Square, millions have marched in open defiance of authorities. The imagination of tens of millions is captured by what President Lincoln described as 'a government of the people, by the people, and for the people'. They are not drawn to democracy because candidates have the ability to collect and spend billions to win elections.

This book is written with the objective of highlighting the challenges facing Indian democracy, especially in relation to the growing role of money in election campaigns. Since 1992, I have gone back to Indian Punjab to observe every state assembly and parliamentary election. Upon my return to Canada after observing the fourteenth assembly elections of Punjab in February 2012, I felt that the electoral process had rapidly degenerated to new lows. It was time to tell the real story. It is not an attempt to raise fingers at individuals or some parties, but highlight the challenges faced by the electoral system to establish legitimate authority. As a result, I decided to alter the names and stories of people at the constituency level in a free-style journalistic manner. The problem, however, is presented in an objective fashion based on my field research and other academic studies. My objective to write an account of the electoral politics of Punjab is a humble effort to tell a story of a phenomenon I have observed for the past two decades. From the role of drugs and alcohol to the role of cash and cult leaders in the dynastic politics of Punjab and India, this story highlights the challenges that limit the ability of the electoral process to establish legitimate authority. It is a story of who does what to whom, when, how and why. The book is divided into nine chapters.

Chapter one focuses on a widely used practice of the distribution of drugs and alcohol in campaigns. It focuses on strategies of individual campaigns to understand the effective use of these substances to build up political support for candidates and parties. It also reveals who is involved in supplying drugs and alcohol to candidates and their campaigns. Furthermore, it cites studies about the impact of the drug/liquor use on the society, in general and the youth, in particular. Finally, the chapter evaluates various policies of the Election Commission to control and end this practice.

Chapter two focuses on the role of caste politics in campaigns. The scope is beyond a simple discussion about the role of reservation in electoral politics. Each party and each individual candidate devise various strategies and tactics to win votes from different caste communities. The chapter largely deals with the effort of candidates to win over Dalit voters in a general category constituency. In this context, the strategies of the Congress, the Akali Dal/BJP and the BSP are discussed with an analytical view of the past elections. The challenge posed by the BSP to the Congress and the efforts made by the Akali Dal/BJP to woo Dalit voters with pro-poor populist programs are analysed with data from 2007 and 2012 elections. The main focus has been to find out whose strategy has succeeded, how and why to win over Dalit voters?

Third chapter examines the institution of dynastic politics in India. It opens with an analysis of the entrenched role of the Nehru-Gandhi family in the Congress Party. It also offers an analysis of how the Congress royal family has maintained a firm grip over the 'honorary Gandhi's' in the state with both 'carrot and stick' policies. This is followed by an analytical perspective into the history of the Akali Dal to reveal how a party of feudal warlords came into the powerful grip of the Badal family of Muktsar. The entire electoral history of the post-independent Punjab is discussed with data to trace the origins of dynastic rule not only at the level of the state but also at the level of a constituency.

Chapter four's main focus is on the emerging alliance between God men and politicians. It offers an analytical perspective on how the powerful Dera chiefs in different parts of Punjab have formed formal and informal alliances with political parties and leaders. It offers insights into the Dera-politician nexus by focusing on three major centers-Dera Sacha Sauda, Dera Sachkhand Balan, and Dera Radha Soami. Furthermore, it gives insights into the modus operandi of some local holy men. In the electoral history of the state, how and why these Godmen have emerged as major power centers.

Chapter five explores the role of media during campaign. It begins with an analytical history of the vernacular press in Punjab, and reveals how the Jalandhar based print media played a vital role in whipping communal sentiments during the Punjabi Suba movement the 1950s and the 1960s, and during the period of the Khalistani insurgency in the 1980s. It offers a critical review of the paid news, in particular of the Gurmukhi and Hindi press. Furthermore, the role of the newly emerged television industry on the electoral politics has been analysed. The chapter offers insights into how objective news simply disappeared during the campaign. It was replaced by paid news by buying the 'packages' from the newspaper owners. It also focuses on the political control over News Channels and the cable network of the state, in particular the monopoly of the Badal family in this business. The role of bureau chiefs and individual journalists from both vernacular and English dailies is also critically reviewed.

The sixth chapter has an analysis of the role of the NRIs in the state election during 2012 campaign. It points to a growing nexus between the criminal underworld of Punjab and the criminal cartels of the NRIs. It reveals how both the domestic and foreign based criminals have found a common cause with the state politicians and government officials. The NRIs not only offer Crores in illegal campaign contributions to individuals and parties but also offer their money laundering services to the corrupt in Punjab-from officials to politicians. Chapter also offers a unique insight into the positive contributions of millions of Indians in the form of remittance to the homeland.

Chapter seven focuses on the rallies and meetings of the Akali Dal in a constituency. It offers insights into the role of the criminal underworld in providing not only drugs and cash but also the muscle power to candidates and parties. It shows how drug cartels have become the backbone of politicians in this border state. With the help of other studies by the scholars, it offers insights on the growing drug trade on the Indo-Pakistan drug and what devastating impact it has had on the health of the youth of Punjab. The profits from these smuggling operations are directed to campaigns and to buy the official connections. Politicians return the favors after getting elected to the corridors of power. Suffice to say: 'he who pays the piper calls the tune.'

Much like chapter seven, the eighth chapter focuses on the rallies and meetings of the Congress in an urban area. It highlights the role of the unsavory individuals in campaigns. The role of who's who of the society's most corrupt and wealthy in the campaign is revealed by looking at the history of individuals and their business operations to explore the 'business-politician' nexus. It shows how those who violate all norms in society to amass wealth support candidates and the parties. For example, an analysis of the role of the owners of the gynecology clinics responsible for the female feticide highlights this connection between the 'business' community and the politicians.

The last chapter begins with the revelations about the origins of the campaign funds and the practice of cash-for-vote. Then it moves on to the whole industry of opinion polling to exit polling agencies to bookies and pundits speculating the winners and losers. Based on the data now available from 2012 election, the study reveals interesting facts and figures to show how the Congress lost the battle of the ballot. It also reveals some key factors that helped the Alkali-BJP coalition during the campaign and helped them to reverse the trend of anti-incumbency in the state. Finally, the analysis also focuses on how a tradition of no respect for the opposition has developed in the state that has offered another challenge to the system of parliamentary democracy. The checks and balances inherent in democracy are on the decline.

In the course of my observations and involvements in various electoral campaigns in Punjab, I met ordinary people, campaign workers, party officials, campaign teams, candidates, party leaders, journalists, researchers, holy men, civic and business leaders, civil and police officials, and, of course, various unsavory characters. It would take a whole chapter to name all of them, but suffice to say that with the exception of the latter, I would like to thank all of the above for their help and trust. It's a remarkable testament to the generosity of Punjabis that after five minutes of initial introduction, they will open their homes for you to stay and live as a family member. They are people with big hearts. I enjoyed this privilege bestowed on me not only from ordinary citizens, but political activists, candidates, and even political leaders of Punjab.

This book, of course, would not have been possible without the help of my family. I lost my father when I was only one month old. I was raised by a single mother. She has dedicated her life to her children. Although she did not attend school for even a day, she encouraged and supported all of us in our studies. Listening to my endless stories about Punjab elections, my wife, Jeetender, encouraged me to write a book telling what really happens during elections. My beautiful daughters, Tavleen, Avneet and Mehtab, created such a wonderful environment at home that I finished the entire book on my laptop at our family dining room table. Needless to say, my daughters inspired my thoughts, my wife appreciated them, and my mother blessed them.

Finally, a word is required about the title of this book. The idea came from China's post-Maoist leadership's claims of building socialism with Chinese characteristics. Deng Hsiao Ping's slogan of 'getting rich is glorious' was certainly different from the Soviet emphasis on 'he who does not work, neither shall he eat.' Similarly, a student of comparative politics will notice how each democracy functions with certain national and cultural characteristics specific to its environment. Living in North America, I have noticed how word Tandoori is associated with everything from India; hence the title- '*Tandoori Democracy*'.

Glossary

Aab	Water
Adivasi	Tribal
Akali	Immortal
Amrit	Bapitization
Atta	Flour
Baba	Elderly, Religious leader
Bahadur	Brave
Bahujan	Majority
Bania	Moneylender
Bet	Surrounding area of river banks
Bhartya	Indian
Bureh	Elderly
Chaa	Tea
Crore	Ten million
Daal	Lentil
Dainik	Daily
Dal	Organisation
Dalit	Untouchable caste
Dera	Abode
Desi	Domestic
Devnagri	Hindi/Punjabi script
Durga	Goddess of Power
Gau Shala	Cow Shelter
Gufa	Cave
Gurdwara	Sikh Temple
Gurmukhi	Punjabi script used by Sikhs
Halwai	Traditional Cook
Harijan	Untouchable caste (name given by Mahatama Gandhi)
Hawaldar	Sergeant

Insan	Human
Jag	World
Jagran	Awakening
Janata	People
Jati	Sub-Caste
Jatt	Landowning Upper Caste
Jawan	Army Private
Jolaha	Weaver
Kabbadi	A traditional Punjabi sport
Kavi	Poet
Kayastha	Caste of Traders, Merchants
Khalistan	Demand for a separate Sikh state
Khalsa	Baptized Sikh
Kirtan	Singing of hymns
Lakh	One hundred thousand
Langar	Community kitchen
Laxmi	Goddess of Wealth
Lok Sabha	Lower house of Indian Parliament
Mandir	Hindu Temple
Mazdoor	Worker
Misl	Sikh Military Formation
Mochi	Cobbler
Mohalewala	Resident of lower caste locality
Nirankari	A Sikh heterodox sect
Pagal	A mentally challenged
Pakora	Fritters
Panchayat	Village Council
Pandit	Brahmin, Priest
Parishad	Association
Pathi	Sikh Priest
Pendu	Villager
Punj	Five
Prabandhik	Management
Radhasoami	A Sikh heterodox sect
Raj	Rule
Roti	Bread
Samachar	News

Samaj	Society
Sangat	Community of worshippers
Sangh	Association
Sardar	Leader, a title used by landowning caste
Sarswati	Goddess of Knowledge
Satsang	Gathering of worshippers
Satya	Truth
Sevadar	Volunteer
Shaheed	Martyr
Shahmukhi	Persian script used by Muslims to write Punjabi
Shaitan	Devil
Sharomani	Supreme
Sarpanch	Village Council Chief
Seva	Volunteer activity
Shagan	Wedding gift
Shamlat	Communal property
Shri	Respected, Honourable
Suba	State (province)
Suraksha	Protection
Vidhan Sabha	State Legislative Assembly
Vidyarthi	Student
Yaar	Friend

1
Whisky-for-Vote

Wine hath drowned more men than the sea
— Thomas Fuller

"One bottle of whisky per vote," said Amar Singh. The suggestion came from the candidate at a late night meeting of the Congress campaign, which focussed on liquor distribution to voters. Almost everyone frowned on the idea. The campaign meeting was late but the issue was so crucial that key members of the Congress team were present in candidate Amar Singh's marble house on this cold and foggy night. They all wanted to impress upon the candidate that the Congress campaign was already falling behind the Akali Dal (a regional Sikh party) campaign in several areas, including liquor distribution to the voters.

In this semi-urban-rural constituency of Dholpur, Amar Singh was facing stiff competition from the Akali Dal candidate and sitting MLA, Jagir Singh. The constituency reflected general trends of Punjab[1] politics in that no incumbent has ever been re-elected from this electoral district of 4 semi-urban towns and 107 villages. As it borders a major river of Punjab, the geographic location of the constituency has made it a major route for smuggling operations. The Dholpur constituency has a population of 224,000, but only 151,000 eligible voters were registered on the electoral list. The fourteenth assembly election in Punjab was scheduled for January 30, 2012, roughly five years after the last assembly election of February 2007. More than 18 million voters from the total state population of 27 million were eligible to vote for a 117 member legislative assembly located in the city of Chandigarh, a joint capital of both Haryana and Punjab. Designed by the French architect, Le Corbusier, and built in the post-independent period, Chandigarh has the distinction of being the newest city of the majority Sikh state where a highly developed *Harappa* civilisation existed in the third millennium before our era. While the Sikhs constituted less than 2 per cent of India's total population compared with the Hindu population of more than 80 per cent, in Punjab they have a majority with little more than 60 per cent of the state's population compared with the Hindu population of 35 per cent. Interestingly, while the Sikhs form a majority in Punjab, they have been a majority only in rural areas. All urban centers of Punjab have a Hindu majority. In the Dholpur constituency, the Sikh voters dominated the electoral list with 66 per cent of the population followed by 32 per cent Hindus and 2 per cent Christians and Muslims. In terms of gender, only 47 per cent of the eligible voters were female and 53 per cent were male. The *Dalit*, or untouchable caste, voters had a significant strength with 26 per cent of the total vote in Dholpur. However, the majority belonged to the landowning *Jatt* Sikh caste with 38 per cent of the eligible voters on the electoral list. Both the Congress and the Akali Dal candidates belonged to this dominant caste of the state[2].

The campaign team of Amar Singh, however, had members from almost all upper castes of Hindus and Sikhs. The team members' loyalty was to Amar Singh, not the Congress Party. As veteran campaigners, some from the days of Amar Singh's father Partap Singh, they were full of ideas. There was a general belief in every campaign that liquor distribution was crucial to remain competitive in elections. No studies have ever shown that offers of liquor garner any electoral support but every campaign team was convinced that liquor distribution was a necessary evil, especially if your opponent was indulging in such practices. The Congress team disagreed with the one bottle idea, and suggested a more liberal distribution of one case (12 bottles of 750 ml) to each household with at least two male voters and two female voters. All eyes then focussed on the treasurer Ram Mohan, who handled campaign finance.

Born and raised in a rural Brahmin family, Ram Mohan was a retired school teacher. In the eyes of the Congress candidate, Mohan was one of the most loyal and trusted members of the team. Mohan was humble and wise. Life and education had taught him important lessons from childhood to this day. He was the youngest in a family of five siblings. His father was a respected priest of a Hindu temple in the village. The villagers simply addressed him as *Pandit-Jee*. A small number of Hindu devotees in the village and changing times meant very little income for the family of a priest. Since *Pandit-Ji* was one of only a handful of villagers who could read and write, he offered free tutoring services for young students. He was also a volunteer letter writer for villagers and offered any other services that required reading and writing. As a result, the villagers shared whatever material goods they produced with this Brahmin family. Despite his father's wishes to educate all his children, only Ram Mohan went to study in a college and graduated with a bachelor of education. As the education system was expanding in newly independent India, Mohan was able to secure a teaching position in a government high school in a nearby town.

Mohan loved his village life and never moved to the town where his school was located. By bicycle, it was a long journey of nine kilometers up and nine kilometers down. "It's good for my health," he used to reason with his friends and colleagues. Like his father, he offered free tutoring services to students and continued this tradition of volunteer service even when almost all teachers had started private tutoring businesses. For some teachers, their tutoring services became so lucrative that they made more money from this business than from their salaries. While students and parents respected Mohan's honesty and work, he was not always in the good books of the school administration.

The school headmaster was a morally and ethically challenged individual. His wife was employed by the school as a 'librarian' but nobody had ever seen her at the institution except during official functions. The library functioned with the help of student 'volunteers'. The Headmaster was also known for siphoning school funds which came for upgrading the labs and other equipment. He accepted bottles of liquor from teachers who had tutoring businesses on the school premises. The Headmaster was however cunning and innovative in achieving high passing grades for students, which pleased both parents and education authorities. He had developed a system of collecting money from students and teachers during exams to offer whisky and other 'entertainment' to invigilators. As a result, students were free to cheat as much as possible without any fear. High passing marks of students indicated that the system produced the desired results. As a teetotaller and an educator with principles, Mohan did not like the offers of liquor to invigilators and refused to help students cheat during exams. Furthermore, he had objected in writing to education authorities that the school facilities were being used by teachers to make money from tuitions.

Mohan remembered his childhood days when social activists used to pay visits to every home to ensure no child of school age was missing from school. The leadership of new India had a vision to enlighten the entire population with public education to build a base for the country's future development. 'If you plan for a year, according a

Chinese proverb, sow rice; if you plan for ten years, plant trees; and if you plan for a hundred years, educate your people'. The fathers of independent India certainly believed in this, but the times had changed. A decade and half long insurgency destroyed this dream for many in the state. Furthermore, the state's new liberalisation program moved away from its commitment to public education and started encouraging the privatization of education. A 2008 study on the state of education in Punjab concluded that 'education in rural Punjab has almost collapsed'[3]. With a drop-out rate of 48 per cent, 69 per cent of rural households in Punjab were without a single family member who had completed grade ten[4]. As the government school system collapsed, the richer segments of the population started shifting their children to private schools. As a result, the government schools now only catered to 'students from *Dalit* and other lower castes'[5].

Ram Mohan had benefited from a public school and college system. He was determined to maintain the quality of education in his school without the additional burden of tuition money. He fought against efforts to lower the standards of education, and elevate costs. In this crusade, he became a thorn in the back of the school Headmaster. In retaliation, the Headmaster used his powers to write poor annual confidential reports about Mohan, and isolated him from other faculty members. The school administration tried every tactic to force Mohan to ask for a transfer from the school. He had the audacity to stand on high moral grounds, but luck was not on his side. The new DEO (district education officer), the Headmaster's old classmate and friend, took over the charge of the district, as the former officer was promoted to the rank of deputy-director. The new officer accepted the Headmaster's recommendation and transferred Mohan to a new school in a border district. Unable to do anything against the power blocs of the education domain, Mohan left his family in his native village and moved to his new place of work in a large village along the India-Pakistan border. He realised that he was a small fish in a corrupt pond. Prime Minister Rajiv Gandhi used to say that only 15 per cent of the government development funds were used for the intended purposes. The remaining 85 per cent was staying in the pockets of political-bureaucratic-business nexuses. As a result, individuals like Mohan were not tolerated in this system. They faced constant harassment for their honesty.

Shifted away to an unknown territory, Mohan had time to reflect on important life lessons. The Sikh militants were virtually ruling the countryside, and no one felt safe in the entire state. Schools were hardly functioning because the diktats of militants made life miserable for students and teachers. Boys who did not wear saffron turbans and girls who did not cover their heads with saffron scarfs were targeted by the militants. Teachers who did not allow cheating were on the hit list of militants. Parents started pulling children out of schools, especially if they had to travel to nearby villages and towns. Ram Mohan's family was worried daily about his safety, and he was worried sick about his family's safety. Under these circumstances, his father took the initiative and contacted the local Congress MLA, Amar Singh's father, Sardar Partap Singh. The MLA used his influence with officials and managed to get Ram Mohan posted in a middle school in his native village. Neither Mohan nor his family ever forgot this favour, and they have remained faithful to this Congress leader's family to date. It was also a new lesson for Mohan. He had to compromise with his puritanical principles. He learned that 'if you live in the river, you should make friends with the crocodile'[6]. His approaching old age and the responsibilities of raising a family forced him into a life of compromise. He was now fit for political life. After retirement, Amar Singh took Mohan into his inner circles on full time basis. Mohan has remained a faithful lieutenant. As a result, Amar Singh assigned him the most important task- money matters. In 2007, however, the Congress candidate faced some book-keeping problems during the assembly campaign, because Mohan was a novice. It had to be corrected with the help of Amar Singh's personal CA (Chartered Accountant). The CA was a sharp man with big dreams. He tried to sideline Mohan for his mistakes. But Amar Singh knew that it's 'better to have a diamond with a few small flaws than a perfect rock'[7]. Thus, his trust in Mohan remained unshaken.

Mohan has never had a drink in his life, but now he was agreeing with other team members to distribute liquor to voters to ensure Amar Singh's victory. Amar Singh, of course, was just testing his team with the 'one bottle' suggestion. He knew how to keep the voters intoxicated during campaigns. He was, however, more concerned about the election commission's guidelines regarding liquor distribution. The Chief Electoral Officer of Punjab, Kusumjit Sidhu, had banned the transportation of liquor at night. During the day time, all vehicles were subject to police/para-military checks all over the state. It was a sincere effort on the part of the Election Commission (EC) to control the use of alcohol to buy votes during elections, but, as with any other law in India, there were those who violated such orders with impunity. Most of these violators were the law makers and the law enforcers.

Ram Mohan informed the team that he had been in touch with the local distiller. The distiller had offered a 75 per cent discount on *Desi* (domestic) whisky. As a result, a bottle would have cost the campaign no more than 20 to 25 '₹' (40 to 50 U.S. cents). The distiller had close relations with the distribution company. Thus, he assured the campaign treasurer that despite the EC's guidelines, the liquor distribution would flow like the mighty Ganga. Although the quality of liquor from this distiller was always questionable, the campaign team was more worried about quantity. Amar Singh had helped the owner of the whisky distillery, Kewal Bhalla, with his license during Congress rule, so it was payback time. However, he was not happy with the idea of a 75 per cent discount. He wanted all free liquor for the campaign and told the team that he would speak with the distillery owner.

Kewal Bhalla grew up in a Hindu *Kayastha* family in a nearby historic town. His father was a small scale shopkeeper and a moneylender. Although his business operations were not on a grand scale by any stretch of the imagination, Bhalla senior still managed to fleece his customers enough to enjoy a middle class lifestyle. Unlike his two younger brothers and an older sister, Kewal did not enjoy studies either in school or in college. His father sent Kewal to college to show neighbours and relatives that all his children were pursuing higher education. It was also important for matrimonial purposes. Kewal stayed in college for seven years in a three year degree course, yet at the end he departed without a diploma in his hands. These years, however, made him street smart beyond the imagination of his father. Kewal was always a worthless parasite in his father's opinion.

Sikh militancy was emerging as the key threat to the peace and security of the region. Colleges and Universities in Punjab witnessed the rise of the AISSF (All India Sikh Student Federation) on all campuses. Many young boys from rural agricultural background with very little land aspired to become soldiers for a new cause-Sikh Homeland. Led by an orthodox Sikh leader, Sant Jarnail Singh Bhinderawale, the movement turned more violent with every passing day. Recruited by the Congress to undermine the Akali party's Sikh base, he became a legend for the Sikh youth[8]. At this crucial moment, Kewal Bhalla became a *Khalsa* Sikh (baptized). While some of his batch mates joined militant organisations, Bhalla remained uncommitted but stayed in contact with his militant friends. Some friends of Bhalla crossed the border to Pakistan to join Sikh militants in training camps of the ISI (Inter Service Intelligence) wing in the Pakistani army. Only one managed to come back, and he was caught and shot dead by Indian paramilitary forces.

Bhalla's role was minor but crucial and profitable. He was a central point for the storing of weapons, and money looted from robberies, hijackings, and ransoms. His family was terrified by the turn of events in his life. Under normal circumstances, A Hindu boy becoming a baptized Sikh was not abnormal. Historically, Hindus of Punjab raised their eldest sons as baptized Sikhs to confront Muslim rulers and invaders. These were, however, different times. Poisonous propaganda from the extreme elements of both Hindu and Sikh communities had created a historic divide that had never existed in Punjab. Thus, Kewal's baptized Sikh status did not go well with family and his close relatives. Undeterred by all of this, he marched on in his chosen path. His close proximity to Sikh militants meant he was able to negotiate ransom deals for kidnapped victims. On the other hand, he had developed close relations with some police and paramilitary officers, an activity only known to a select few in his circles. Thus, he was able to negotiate the release of many suspected militants. In these transactions, he was making money from both sides. He also 'arranged' the 'arrest' of several militants who later joined the police counter-insurgency operations against terrorists.

As militancy ended in Punjab in 1993, Bhalla became a clean-shaven gentleman. He turned his attention to property business in two of the most populated cities in Punjab- Jalandhar and Ludhiana. Bhalla had a flow of cash, friendship with goon-squads, and links to police officials. This deadly combination made him rich beyond anyone's belief. Initially, his main property business was aimed at (NRIs) Non-Resident Indians. Many NRIs had urban properties rented to individuals, who refused to vacate. Afraid of coming back because of militancy, NRIs were willing to transfer their properties to Bhalla's name at a fraction of the market value. Thanks to Bhalla's several ex-militant friends now settled in several western nations, he was able to pay NRIs in the currency of their choice in their domicile country. As the business flourished, he turned his attention to politics. Election to the corridors of law-making bodies meant authorities would not be able to touch your ill-gotten wealth. He paid money to several powerful leaders in the party, but at the end BJP's selection committee refused to nominate him as their candidate. He turned his intention to big business, and secured a liquor distillery license. Since Amar Singh had played a crucial role in this process of obtaining a license, Bhalla had promised to back him with cash and any other services.

Offers of cash and services always came from all business people to all major political parties in Punjab, as the license permit raj and inspector raj continued to play havoc on the 'free enterprise economy'. In return, the business houses got exemptions from labour and environmental laws, and faced no punishment for evading taxes. The liquor industry was even more crucial in the mutually beneficial system. It has been a major source of revenue for the Punjab government. In the 2010-11 fiscal year, excise duty alone from liquor sales brought Rs. 3190.49 *Crores* (nearly 32 billion) to treasury coffers[9]. The state government has also been making huge amounts of money from selling permits through a lottery system to all liquor vendors in Punjab and to liquor distribution companies that buy directly from distilleries and supply to vendors. Addicted to tax revenues coming from the sale of alcohol in the state, the government has a vested interest in promoting the use of liquor. The revenue from this source has been used to balance expenditures on subsidies offered to buy votes of various segments of the population.

Punjab has been second only to Kerala in per capita alcohol consumption in India[10]. In recent elections, liquor distribution to voters has become as important as promising the moon in election manifestos of the political parties. Perhaps the voters were only able to see that imaginary moon of political manifestos in the state of intoxication. From the time of Prime Minister Indra Gandhi, the Congress has been promising to 'eradicate poverty' from rural and urban India. Unable to remove poverty, the Congress has been more successful in removing the poor from their lands and natural habitats to pave the way for private investments. The Akali Dal had launched *Dharm Yudh Morcha* (Agitation to protect religion) with a demand to reduce the powers of central government and concentrate almost all powers in state jurisdiction[11] in a highly decentralized federation. After several years of bloodshed, the Akali Dal has finally stopped making any references to its demand for 'more powers to states'. In the meantime, its leader, Parkash Singh Badal, has managed to concentrate all party powers in the hands of his family.

The story of widespread liquor distribution, however, to voters in Punjab has been less than two decades old. In 'good old times,' the only liquor distribution was to key campaign workers, so they could end their days in a lighter mood. Even that was not done from a candidate's campaign office. Normally key supporters of the candidate provided volunteers for the campaign, and they took care of the spiritual and material needs of these foot-soldiers. Beginning in the mid-nineties, as Punjab emerged from the dark days of terrorist violence and police excesses, the political parties started outdoing each other to capture the executive power in the state. It has become such an evil that now the Election Commission was under pressure from enlightened elements in the society to ban such practices.

The ban on the transportation of liquor by the EC at night time produced some results. The officials seized 3,797 litres of illicit liquor, 92,742 locally made bottles of wine, 8580 kilograms of opium and 157241 tablets of narcotics[12] in the first few days of the campaign. Unfortunately, these seizures were only the tip of the iceberg. From all 30 liquor distilleries of Punjab, some 180 trucks carried 400 cases of whisky each to local vendors and candidates on a daily basis. This translated to 72,000 cases each containing 12 bottles of whisky for a total of 864,000 bottles. Furthermore, it was estimated that the country made illicit liquor has a market share equal to the branded market[13] . Thus, Punjab's 18 million electors had access to nearly two million bottles of whisky per day from state's internal sources alone. Distilleries located in the bordering states of Haryana, Himachal and Rajasthan also supplied huge amounts of liquor to Punjab, especially during election campaigns.

Election Commission's *diktats* had a psychological impact on all campaigns. Even in material terms all efforts were not in vain, especially where candidates chose to openly defy these orders in broad day lights, and opposition candidates complained to the authorities at the opportune moments. A case was registered against Bibi Jagir Kaur, a major Akali leader, who was also accused of killing her own daughter, for supply of alcohol to her constituents. Her Congress opponent, Sukhpal Singh Khaira, had complained to EC that this former President of Sharomani Gurdwara Prabandhak Committee (SGPC-known as mini-Sikh Parliament) and head of a religious *Dera* (abode) of *Labana* Sikh community had 183 cases of whisky ready for distribution to voters[14]. Legally, it had no impact on Bibi's candidacy, but it exposed her religious veneer. In the adjacent constituency of Kapurthala, the authorities seized some 7,000 cases of liquor from the Congress candidate Rana Gurjit Singh's campaign.[15] Since Rana owned a liquor distillery, the replacement of seized liquor was just a minor inconvenience.

Realizing the publicity for liquor distribution did not go well for campaigns, candidate Amar Singh was simply being cautious. He knew how to circumvent the EC's orders, but as a veteran of state politics, he wanted to maintain a 'clean image'. There were many among Punjab politicians who held the view that liquor controversy was a free advertisement. This kind of news informed voters in their electoral district that liquor was available from the candidate's campaign. Amar Singh did not subscribe to this view because almost all women voters despised the practice of free liquor distribution. Even in the previous campaign, the women had objected to the gatherings organized in villages and towns by campaign workers which provided unlimited quantity of liquor and appetizers to their husbands. As victims of beatings at the hands of their drunken husbands, the women voters understandably had a negative view of the practice of liquor distribution. Although Indians have a saying, 'never strike your wife, not even with a flower'[16], the practice, however, has always been different.

Another urgent issue for the Congress candidate was the distribution of drugs. The leader of a smuggling gang had agreed to provide methamphetamine pills and other drugs for free. However, he was reluctant to say yes to heroin because it was very expensive. A big transporter had agreed to bring poppy husk and opium from the state of Uttar Pradesh to distribute among the addicts. Although most male voters were happy with this arrangement of free liquor and drugs, the campaign also witnessed pockets of resistance. Youth in many cities and towns had formed groups to stop the distribution of drugs and liquor during the campaign 2012. They had a reason because the youth of Punjab had suffered a great deal from drugs and alcohol. A study conducted by the Institute of Development Communication (IDC) and Guru Nanak Dev University (Amritsar) estimated that 70 per cent of Punjab's youth were addicted to alcohol or drugs[17].

Focused on just winning the executive power, politicians were not concerned with the disastrous impact of their actions on the youth or on any other segment of the population. Elections have become wars but without tanks and fighter jets. Neither war nor electoral battles produced any second place winners. In short, there were no silver medals in politics. With single-mindedness of purpose to win this assembly seat, the Congress team finalized all aspects of liquor and drugs strategies and decided to take a cautious approach. All vehicles carrying liquor were to have two escort cars, one two miles ahead to caution about any police checkpoints and one just behind the main vehicle to ensure no one had been tailgating them. Mobile phones were finally becoming handy to break the law with impunity.

In towns, elected Congress councillors and other stalwarts friendly to the Congress candidate were to lead the charge of storage and distribution. In villages, liquor and drugs were to be distributed daily on the basis of need because storage was more difficult in places where everybody knew each other's names. The most trusted people were to be in charge of this operation, and in case of police seizure, they would take the responsibility and protect the candidate. The most difficult question was how to proceed in the *Bet* area (surroundings of the River) because people in this area privately produced illicit country made liquor. The suggestion came to supply them with molasses based on per family vote count, so they could make their own liquor. A brilliant idea but its effectiveness was questionable. The area residents were upset that during Congress rule, they were constantly raided and harassed by police.

Democracy presented a strange puzzle to the political class. The multi-billionaire lobby of liquor distillers, distributers and liquor store vendors had been lobbying to authorities to eliminate illicit liquor production and distribution because it snatched away a significant portion of the market from legal entities, which provided a huge tax base for the state coffers. On the other hand, a significant portion of electors in constituencies bordering all rivers in Punjab were heavily involved in illicit liquor production and distribution. During election times, the support of this segment could tilt the balance in many electoral districts. As Bet area residents were not happy with Congress government's 'heavy-handedness', the Akali candidate had made a deal with the locals to ensure 'immunity' from police and excise department raids in the last election. He won and the Akali Dal took over the executive in coalition with the BJP in 2007. The Akali MLA kept his word but only partially. While his staunch supporters enjoyed 'immunity', the people who did not openly support his candidacy were harassed and humiliated. Thus, a section of *Bet* area residents were ready to support the Congress, if a deal could be reached.

Amar Singh was urged to meet with Kishan. Kishan Singh was the acknowledged leader of the disgruntled segment of Bet area residents. He was known in his area for his body and mental strength. In his early 40s, he could still wrestle a male buffalo to the ground. For generations, his family had only known two businesses: agriculture and illicit liquor. Living on the banks of a major river meant agriculture was at the mercy of nature, especially during monsoon season. At best, the area residents could only count on one crop while two or even three crops were common in the rest of the state. Liquor business was more profitable except during the raids by police and excise officials. As there was no school in the surrounding area during his childhood, Kishan remained illiterate. He was tall, well-built, and fearless. He could outrun any police party and swim faster than alligators. Thus, during police raids, he always escaped from being arrested. Then police changed its tactics and nabbed him during pre-dawn raids when Kishan was still asleep.

Kishan's police and court records became lengthy, and, at every opportune moment, police raided his premises to put pressure on his family business. His elder son came to his rescue at crucial times. Built like his father, Tota hardly studied during his school days in a new government school in the village. He was of the opinion that education was for the physically weak, those who were unable to perform hard labour. When he was not busy with sports, Tota was either stealing or perfecting his liquor making skills. He became friendly with police for his culinary skills of making finest chicken curry from stolen birds. Local *Hawaldar* (sergeant) and constables could always count on Tota's fine liquor and spicy chicken for evening gatherings. As a result, Tota was also able to influence police raids to keep his father out of trouble. Kishan, however, was made of different stuff. If not in liquor troubles, he was involved in almost every other conflict in his village and the surrounding area. A self-proclaimed truth seeker, Kishan always sided with the weak party. His friends admired him for his two basic qualities: speaking the truth and keeping his word. When the Akali candidate made a deal with the villagers during last election, Kishan was happy to support him. The situation took a U-turn as soon as he saw his arch rival from the village sitting next to the candidate during an election rally. Not politically savvy, Kishan started supporting a local independent candidate who ended up with 789 votes from a total of 115,000 polled on election-day. A bitter lesson but now Kishan was willing to support a candidate from a major party.

Amar Singh knew that his primary strength came from the support base of the Congress Party. In addition, the family's dynastic electoral history had created pockets of influence all over the constituency. To win, he also needed the support of the disgruntled elements from the ranks of the opposition. Every election was decided by a few swing voters. They were most demanding and difficult to read. Amar Singh knew that going back to *Bet* area and making deals with illicit liquor distillers was not an easy task, but he had no other option. He agreed to meet Kishan as soon as possible. Times were calling for broadening the base of the Congress support. Nothing creates closer social bonds than an intoxicated state of mind. As the meeting ended and everyone rose to leave the house, Amar Singh was quick to remind them to start "liquor distribution immediately to *Mohalewalas* (Lower Caste localities)."

References

1.   *Punj* means five; and *aab* means water. The name Punjab means the land of five rivers: Jhelum, Chenab, Ravi, Beas and Satluj.

2. All population related data is taken from Shinder Purewal (2000). *Sikh Ethno nationalism and the Political Economy of Punjab.* New Delhi: Oxford University Press, pp. 3-6.
3. Ranjit S. Ghuman (2008). Socio-Economic Crisis in Rural Punjab. *Economic and Political Weekly*, Vol. 43 (6), p. 13.
4. *Ibid.,* p. 14.
5. *Ibid.*, p. 13.
6. An Indian proverb.
7. *Ibid.*
8. See Kuldip Nayar and Khushwant Singh (1984). *Tragedy of the Punjab: Operation Bluestar and after.* New Delhi: Vikas.
9. *The Economic Times*, January 17, 2012.
10. *The Times of India*, March 30, 2012.
11. The Akali Dal passed the Anandpur Sahib Resolution in 1973 demanding all powers to states except foreign affairs, defence, currency and communication. For a critical analysis of this resolution, see Shinder Purewal (2000). op. ci pp. 87-89.
12. *The Economic Times*, January 17, 2012.
13. *Ibid.*
14. *Ibid.*
15. *The Tribune,* June 28, 2012.
16. An Indian Proverb.
17. *Ibid.*

2

The Caste Campaign

But for the sake of the prosperity of the worlds, He caused the Brahmana, the Kshatriya, the Vaisya, and the Sudra to proceed from his mouth, his arms, his thighs and his feet

*– **Manu Smriti***

One of the key indicator of voting behaviour in Punjab has been the caste affiliation. Akali candidate Jagir Singh understood it very well. The main objective of this very early morning drive to a *Dalit* ('untouchable' caste) supporter's house in the thick fog was to update strategy toward 'lower caste' voters. Known simply as 'Sarpanch' (Village Council Chief), the *Dalit* supporter in question belonged to the Dholpur constituency's largest village with more than 4200 votes. In fact, the real Sarpanch was his wife, who was elected as the head of the village Council (known as *Panchayat*) in the last election with Jagir Singh's help. On a rotational electoral reservation system, the village came in the quota system for *Dalit* women. The 73rd amendment entrenched the *Panchayati Raj* in the constitution, which has given 33 per cent reservation to women, and a certain percentage to *Dalits* according to their share of the state's population. In this patriarchal system, even when women were elected heads of village councils, their husbands became de facto heads carrying out all the official functions. It was the same story with this *Dalit Sarpanch*.

Coming from a landless 'untouchable' family, the Sarpanch has done very well for himself and his family. For the past few years, he has lived in a marble house located in his ten acre farm on the east side of the village. The village was a typical round shaped locality with ancient settings. It has five large gates of entry as was necessary in the days of regular invasions from Alexander the Great to the Afghans. All higher castes lived in the center of the village surrounded by intermediate and artisan castes. Untouchables were never allowed to settle inside the walled villages. Moreover, they were also not allowed to have colonies in the East side because the sunrise was considered sacred. During nights, the gates were closed out of fear of robbers and thieves. They were permanently closed during invasions. Untouchables enjoyed no protection because they had no material wealth for robbers and invaders. A large *Mandir* (Hindu Temple) and a *Gurdwara* (Sikh Temple) were also located in the center of the village. The only Mosque located near the western gate lied in ruins because the entire Muslim population of this village shifted to Pakistan during 1947 partition. A 'modern' Guru lived outside the village in his massive '*Gufa*' (cave) built by granite stone brought from the state of Rajasthan. His claim to fame was his 'effort' to eradicate the caste system and offer a new path of 'enlightenment'. He accepted donations from all castes, but refused to eat food prepared by the *Dalits*.

Caste is a Portuguese word used to explain India's *Verna* (literally skin colour) system. Ancient Indian religious tradition claimed that society could function properly only if all classes performed duties assigned to them by their birth in the *Verna* system. By this account, the *Brahmans*, who came from the Lord's mouth, were responsible for performing religious prayers, learning, teaching and studying. The *Kshatrya*, who came from the Lord's arms, were responsible for the protection of the society, as warriors and Kings. The *Vaishya*, who came from the thighs of the Lord, were responsible for material aspects of life like trade, commerce and agriculture. The *Sudra*, who came from the Lord's feet, were responsible for all services to the twice-born higher castes[1]. There was, however, no mention of untouchables in ancient *Vedas*. The category of outcastes developed over time to denote a status of inferiority to those who cleaned sewers and tended to dead animals. There have been numerous debates on the origins of untouchability, but suffice to say that untouchables, as the lowest layer of this social pyramid, were treated worse than animals and slaves for centuries.

A traveller to India would not be able to find the caste system in this clear cut four *Verna* system in any part of the sub-continent. Instead, one would find hundreds of *Jatis,* castes arranged by their occupations, all over India. These *Jatis* would then be arranged within the framework of the original four or five *Verna* system into the highest, the intermediate, the lower, and the lowest castes (the untouchables). In Punjab, the most dominant caste has been the *Jatt* Sikhs-landowners and warriors[2]. They are numerically, economically, socially and politically the most dominant group in the countryside, representing roughly one-third of the state's population³ (half of the rural population because two third of Punjab's population lives in the villages). The *Brahmins* and *Kayathas* form the upper layer of the Hindu caste pyramid in Punjab, the members of which mainly reside in urban centers where one-third of the state's population lives. The *Kayasthas* are divided into both religions the Hindu and Sikh. There are numerous inter-mediate castes in both villages and cities, which include the *Banias, Kambos, Sainis, Labanas, Tarkhans, Lohars, Suniaras, Gujjars* and others. Among the members of the lower castes are *Kalals, Chimbas, Jhewers, Naees* and others. The lowest (Dalits) among the castes of Punjab are *Chuhras* (Scavengers, also known as *Balmiki, Bhangi,* and *Mazhbi*) who largely converted to Sikhism, and *Chamars* (Cobblers, also known as *Harijans, Ravidasi, Adharmi* and *Mochi)* who have remained mainly in the fold of Hindu society. Constitutionally known as SCs (as they are listed in a special schedule of castes attached to the constitution), the *Dalits* constitute around 29 per cent of the state's population.

Akali candidate Jagir Singh firmly believed that the majority of the *Jatt* Sikhs would vote for his party. In 2007, the Akali Dal got the support of 60 per cent of voters belonging to the *Jatt* Sikh community⁴. This feeling was shared by the Congress candidate Amar Singh who believed that *Jatt* Sikhs were hoodwinked to support the regional party by its policies of free electricity to run tube-wells to irrigate the crops. Jagir Singh also believed that upper caste *Brahmins* and *Kayathas* would support his candidacy because the Akali Dal had an electoral alliance with the BJP. The record from the 2007 assembly election indicated that the Akali-BJP coalition enjoyed more support among Hindu upper caste voters for a total of 48 per cent compared with 43 per cent for the Congress. However, there was no doubt that most of this vote was cast for the BJP candidates in major urban centers. In the absence of a BJP candidate, some of this upper caste Hindu vote was going to shift to the Congress. At least, that was what Amar Singh had told his supporters. The intermediate castes presented a real battlefield, as there were no major known candidates from these communities except one. The People's Party of Punjab (PPP) had fielded a *Bania* (moneylender caste) as their candidate. For Jagir Singh, the real challenge came from *Harijan* voters. Two major sub-castes of *Dalits*, the *Balmikis* and the *Harijans*, have divided political loyalties. Although Akali-BJP secured a sizeable portion of the vote from both the Hindu and Sikh Dalits in 2007 with 29 per cent and 30 per cent respectively, there was no doubt that the Congress was always the favourite of Dalits. Even with the rise of the *Dalit* led BSP (Bahujan Samaj Party), the Congress managed

to secure 51 per cent of the *Dalit* Sikh vote and 37 per cent of the
Hindu *Dalit* vote in 2007. Despite its' openly pro-*Dalit* agenda, the
BSP was able to secure only about 12 per cent of the votes among the
Hindu and Sikh Dalits in 2007. The Akali candidate Jagir Singh was
still convinced that the rise of the BSP vote was more damaging to the
Congress than the Akali Dal. He had a strong base among the *Balmiki
Dalit* community; thus, Jagir Singh calculated that he could offer direct
competition to his opponent in this community. However, his strategy
of denying the Congress its vote bank among the *Harijans* depended
heavily on the success of the BSP campaign[5].

As a result, Jagir Singh's early morning meeting at Sarpanch's house
was very crucial to deal with the *Dalit* strategy. Sarpanch had grown up
in this village, and by virtue of his position, as husband of village council
head, he carried a certain aura of power. Now a staunch supporter of the
Akali Dal, Sarpanch had served in the ranks of other parties and groups,
including the BSP. He was born in a *Harijan* family. His father was a farm
labourer and a simple man who believed in *Dharma*. If one worked hard
and performed the assigned duties of the caste in this life, he believed,
one's next life would be better. Sarpanch, however, was cast from a
different mold. Number five of his nine siblings, with four brothers and
five sisters, he studied in the village government school with boys of other
castes. Family poverty forced him out of school in grade 10, but he had
acquired the basic skills to lead a better life than his parents. In school,
he was heavily influenced by the Communist ideology of his Punjabi
teacher. He joined the ranks of the Communist Youth wing and started
working as a labour organizer in the farm sector. His father did not like
this activism against the power blocs of the village, but *Sarpanch* had
his siblings and other *Dalit* youth of the village on his side. They were
also backed by the upper caste activists of the youth and student wings
of the Communist movement. A strike for higher wages by *Dalit* farm
labour, however, created a wedge in this cross-caste unity because the
sons of landowning *Jatt* Sikhs started backing their families in this 'class
struggle.' *Dalits* led by young Communist activists decided to go on an
indefinite strike in support of their demands. The upper caste landlords
formed a united front and passed an order not to allow farm labourers in
their lands even to-relieve themselves. As there were no toilets in *Dalit*
homes, this call had the greatest impact on their immediate lives.

The strike ended before the dusk, but serious damage was done to
the ranks of Communist unity. From now on, they were divided between
the upper and lower caste cadres. The movement was further weekend

by the emergence of Sikh militancy. The rank and file of Sikh militants was filled with largely *Jatt* Sikh boys ranging from small to medium farms. The village scene changed as para-military forces arrived to suppress militancy. It had a huge impact on Sarpanch's life. Largely to settle old scores from village politics, Sikh militants from this village started targeting the *Sarpanch* and his *Dalit* friends. An attack on his house left his youngest brother in a coma, but this increased his resolve to 'fight' militancy. The Communist Party's leadership came to fully back him and they recommended his name for armed security guards. *Sarpanch* became a police informer earning further wrath of Sikh militants. These events also changed his financial circumstances. In the law of the jungle that prevailed during the days of militancy, both sides of the counter-insurgency-the militants and the state forces- made windfall profits. The price, however, was heavy for civilians as thousands died in this senseless violence. Extra powers given to security forces to deal with this militancy also meant extra-corruption and extra-killings. Families of young men arrested by police were willing to pay any amount for the release and safety of their sons. As a middle man in the bribery cycle of police and para-military forces, Sarpanch was able to pocket large amounts of money.

At the peak of the battle between the militants and the security forces, the government of Narsimha Rao decided to hold assembly elections in Punjab in 1992. Prime Minister Rao was determined to put an end to militancy in Punjab and restore normalcy. He was convinced that only a popularly elected government would be able to guide the security operations in the state, on the one hand, and win the minds and hearts of the population, on the other. Now a rich man with important links, *Sarpanch* applied for nomination seeking the Communist Party ticket from Dholpur. He was denied the party nomination on the basis of his caste. Dholpur was not reserved for SC candidates; therefore, the party could not nominate a *Harijan* from a general category seat. The concept of reservation was part of social engineering attempted by fathers of new India to uplift previously underprivileged groups. It was initially slated for ten years, but it has continued beyond its various expiry dates[6]. Fully 84 parliamentary seats have been reserved for members of the *Dalit* community in the Indian parliament of 543 elected members. Fifteen per cent of all government jobs and seats in government colleges and universities have also been reserved for candidates from SC background. In the newly demarcated boundaries of Punjab, thirty-four seats were reserved for *Dalits* from a total of 117 in the assembly.

Denied nomination of his own party, *Sarpanch* resigned from the primary membership of the Communist Party and denounced its leadership. "Isn't it ironic that the party that denounces the caste system as religious and feudal has the same caste based guidelines to nominate candidates as other parties," he told his supporters. In his angry tone, he also pointed out that the entire party leadership belonged to the upper castes, and also that there has never been a Dalit leader of any Communist group in India. His banner of revolt was damaging to the Communist party, but its leadership refused to reconsider the nomination process. Sarpanch decided to declare his candidacy as an independent. As the elections were boycotted by the militants and major Akali factions, the turn-out was dismal with only around 19 per cent of voters of Dholpur exercising their right to vote. Militants had threatened to kill anyone who dared to vote and as a result most of the voting took place in towns and cities where security forces were present in large numbers. Some villages did not record a single vote. The Congress candidate Amar Singh won the election with little effort. Sarpanch received only 79 votes, but he was happy that his name was now well-known all over the area.

The newly formed government of Sardar Beant Singh moved quickly to crush Sikh militancy backed by Pakistani ISI and the state[7]. Within a year, normalcy was restored in Punjab. As life security returned, *Sarpanch* bought a few acres of land from his village NRI, who had settled in the United Kingdom. He also built a farm house in the newly purchased land. He pulled his sons and daughter from village government school and enrolled them in an English medium school in the city. He was quick to make use of his ill-gotten money as property values started soaring in peaceful Punjab. As his economic status improved, he received an offer from the BSP he could not refuse. He was appointed general-secretary in the sub-district unit of the party. The honeymoon did not last. As the BSP did not give him the nomination in the 1997 assembly elections, he decided to go with a splinter group. He soon realized that this splinter group from the BSP was a one man show. *Sarpanch* had to fish somewhere else and he landed in the pond of the Akali Dal. After winning the assembly seat with a large margin, the Akali MLA Jagir Singh approached the Sarpanch for an alliance. Sarpanch was ready to play an associate's role for the governing party MLA. He was given a respected place in the constituency level party organisation and access to civil and police officials for any work. For five years, *Sarpanch* lived on cloud nine.

In the 2002 assembly election, Jagir Singh lost to Congress candidate Amar Singh. The Congress was back in power under the leadership of Captain Amarinder Singh. *Sarpanch* would have flipped to the Congress but he had earned the wrath of a state level Congress leader during the days of militancy. Accompanied by a major Congress Dalit leader of Punjab, *Sarpanch* had an opportunity to visit the home of this state level Congress leader in Chandigarh. As they entered the Congress leader's house, *Sarpanch* witnessed the presence of Free Khalistan chief- a known terrorist. The chief suddenly moved inside, but *Sarpanch* recognized him because he was from a nearby small village. As they came back, *Sarpanch* was told to maintain silence about this episode. A few days later, a deadly attack on *Sarpanch*'s house convinced him that he would be silenced and nobody would ever hear about this story. He decided to tell everyone, including members of the journalistic community. As stories appeared in the press, the Congress leader denied these 'fictitious stories concocted by the opposition.' However, he never forgot, and vetoed *Sarpanch*'s entry in the ranks of the Congress.

Five years of Congress rule meant three trumped up charges in criminal cases, and loss of money. However, *Sarpanch* now had no option but to stick around Jagir Singh's inner circles. 'Certain bad luck', according to a Chinese proverb, 'is actually a blessing in disguise'. 'Loyalty' paid off as Jagir Singh won back the assembly seat from Congress in 2007 and became a Parliamentary Secretary in the Akali government led by Sardar Parkash Singh Badal. From his personal experience with law and order machinery, *Sarpanch* learned new tactics of intimidation-false charges against opponents. He became an important member of Jagir Singh's team to intimidate and subdue opponents. *Sarpanch*'s speciality was the misuse of Scheduled Castes and Scheduled Tribes (Prevention of Atrocities-SC-ST/POA) Act, 1989. Section 3 of the Act deals with derogatory language used against the untouchables. In the context of Punjab's caste system, calling *Chuhra* or *Chamar* to members of *Balmiki* or *Harijan* communities respectively with an intent to insult or humiliate them amounted to an offence under the provisions of SC-ST/POA Act. *Sarpanch*'s task was to produce affidavits from members of the untouchable castes stating that a member of a higher caste had used derogatory language to insult them in public. It was enough to bring many political opponents and 'enemies' under control because the police force was taking orders only from the Akali leaders controlling the state executive.

The abuse of this law was not limited to Punjab. The provisions of this Act have been widely misused all over the country. An Additional Sessions Judge of Delhi remarked that "unfortunately one comes across growing instances of cases where the provisions of this Act [SC-ST/ POA- S.P.] have not been invoked for the betterment of those it seeks to protect, but by those who want to settle personal scores."[8] Noticing a tendency of growing false cases even in the appeals courts, a Punjab and Haryana High Court Judge, Justice Sullar observed: "As strange as it may appear, but strictly speaking, the common tendency and the frequency of complaints of involving and roping the accused on vague and bold allegations under section 3 of the Act, have been tremendously increasing day by day in our society....This tendency needs to be curbed. If not discouraged…it will ultimately weaken those true cases of prosecution…and the very object and the purpose of the Act would pale into insignificance."[9] Despite warnings from the courts and stories in the media, the industry of the false cases has continued to flourish.

As an expert in 'law', *Sarpanch* became a reliable source for silencing Jagir Singh's opponents. Jagir Singh not only encouraged *Sarpanch*, but also advised him to even help some Akali leaders in other constituencies. *Sarpanch* forgot a cardinal rule: 'Beware of the person who gives you advice according to his own interest'[10]. He became dizzy with success and started playing with fire. Upon Jagir Singh's advice, he became involved in a case against the powerful Dhillon brothers of the area. A wealthy *Jatt* Sikh landlord family of Dhillon brothers was emerging as a major challenge to Jagir Singh within the ranks of the Akali Dal. All politicians have friends and supporters, opponents and enemies. Friends are often a small circle of personal acquaintances. They will support a public figure regardless of his political affiliation. The supporters come from party ranks; and their numbers increase with victories and growing political clout and dwindle with defeats and falling political fortunes. The opponents are members of other parties who offer opposition in the electoral domain and present a choice to voters in the democratic process. The enemies, however, come from the ranks of one's own party. For Jagir Singh, the emerging enemies were the Dhillon brothers. They were simply known as such because of the family's internal unity. Two brothers had settled in the United States, and three lived in the electoral district of Dholpur with their extended families. The secret of family unity, according to Dhillon senior, was ensuring personal space for each family member. Every male child was moved to his own house shortly after his marriage. While the family farm and other business operations remained collective property, each member was at liberty in his own house. Dhillons had proven to others that 'a family is like a forest, when you are outside, it's dense, and when you are inside you see that each tree has its place'[11]. Observing this granite like internal family unity, some people in private called them the Dhillon mafia.

Jagir Singh was particularly concerned about the youngest Dhillon and his close proximity with senior leaders of the Akali Dal. Together with *Sarpanch*, Jagir Singh and his sons hatched-up a conspiracy to sideline their opponents. After paying a huge amount of money, *Sarpanch* produced affidavits from two untouchable female labourers from the Dhillon farm alleging attempted rape and use of derogatory language by the youngest Dhillon. As the local MLA had clout, the police registered a case and the story appeared in the news media the very next day. The Dhillon brothers had money and muscle power, but no one had ever dared challenge their moral character. They were known for showing respect to everyone, especially women. *Sarpanch* had ignored the history of the Dhillon clan. As they say, 'If you close your eyes to facts, you will learn through accidents'[12]. As the story spread, two members of the young Dhillon clan, along with their friends, abducted *Sarpanch* and his elder son. They were taken to a secluded place and tortured. Shots were fired in each knee cap of both the father and son. The injured bodies were dumped near a hospital. Needless to say, the cases against the Dhillon family members were immediately withdrawn along with a personal written apology from *Sarpanch*. The father and son survived but they were crippled for life. The Dhillon case was *Sarpanch*'s last case of producing affidavits for false accusations against anyone. He had learned an important lesson: 'don't look where you fell, but where you slipped'[13]. Walking on crutches, *Sarpanch* continued to support Jagir Singh because he was now totally dependent on the Akali leader's support.

Jagir Singh's entourage arrived at *Sarpanch*'s house. Normally, he would stand on the main road to receive his VIP guests, but now *Sarpanch* was only able to come to the front door of his house. Immediately, they both moved into a small room on the ground floor of the house, as the rest of the campaign team sat down in the main drawing room for a catered breakfast while the drivers and the security guards were standing in the garden. It was a cold morning, but thanks to the election process, all villages, towns and cities were provided twenty four hours of electric power by the state controlled electricity board. Under normal circumstances, no one can ever count on electricity, especially during summer and winter months when the demand for power reaches its zenith. *Sarpanch*'s house was making full use of power stolen directly from the electrical wires passing in front of his property. The Villagers call it *Kundi* (stealing power), and the *Sarpanch* was not alone in this robbery of state exchequer. The heaters were on full blast not only inside this spacious house, but also in the open garden. Jagir Singh, however, cared less about this artificial heat than about the heat of the campaign.

Since Dalits constituted more than a quarter of Dholpur's vote bank, the Akali candidate was interested to hear *Sarpanch*'s analysis. He trusted this old horse of *Dalit* politics. Unlike many other sycophants, *Sarpanch* did not exaggerate the figures. It was not uncommon for politicians to meet people who would claim to deliver hundreds if not thousands of votes. *Sarpanch* was careful with his words and began on a positive note. "Our *Atta* (flour) and *Daal* (pulses) scheme," said *Sarpanch*, "has attracted a lot of attention among *Dalit* voters". The scheme was launched during the 2007 assembly campaign as the key promise by the Akali Dal to attract the votes of poor segments of the population. It had promised thirty five kilograms of wheat and four kilograms of pulses on a monthly basis at a subsidized rate of ₹ 4 and ₹ 20 per kilogram respectively to every family living under the poverty line. The scheme eventually covered some 16 Lakh (1.6 million) families, but the amount of wheat and pulses were reduced to 25 kilograms and 2.5 kilograms respectively[14]. Another popular Akali scheme was a *Shagun* (gift) of ₹ 15,000 to poor girls at the time of their weddings. An old central scheme was revived by the Akali Dal before election call to provide bicycles to female students studying in grades eleven and twelve who had to travel more than 2.5 kilometers to attend school. In *Sarpanch*'s view, all these populist schemes were attractive to the poor *Dalit* voters. In this election, the Congress had upped the ante by offering wheat at even cheaper rate of only ₹ 1 per kilogram. The Akali leadership was quick to counter this populist measure by offers of doubling the *Shagun* money to ₹ 30,000, plus offers of free lap-tops for grade 12 students, free education to all girls up to grade 12, free medical insurance for the poor up to ₹ 200,000, and free 5-*Marla* plots (30 square yards) to landless poor[15].

Democracy brought attention to all segments of the population because each vote was important. It also broke down identity barriers, *albeit* only in terms of voting behaviour, as people voted for different priorities. Although *Dalits* were always seen as Congress supporters, the populist measures of BJP-Akali government attracted the poor segments to the platform of parties with alleged bias toward upper caste landlords, traders, and industrialists. *Sarpanch* knew that the party had come a long way to attract poor *Dalits* and migrant labourers with 'subsidy politics', but he was still cautious in overestimating the Akali strength. Since *Dalits* in Punjab were divided between the *Harijan* and *Balmiki* communities, the voting behaviour was also divided. *Sarpanch* was confident that the *Balmiki* community's vote would split evenly between the Congress and the Akali Dal, but the majority of *Harijans* would vote for the Congress followed by the BSP candidate Prem Lal Bains. Sarpanch advised Jagir Singh that the strategy should be to split the non-BSP Harijan vote evenly between the Congress and the Akali Dal. "The coalition of BJP/Akali Dal with its populist pro-poor policies had the ability to attract enough *Dalit* vote to meet the Congress challenge," said *Sarpanch*. "However, the hard core vote of *Dalits* would go to the BSP".

The BSP was founded by a Punjabi *Dalit*, Kanshi Ram, in 1984. A low level employee of the DRDO (Defence Research and Development Organisation), Kanshi Ram was an active trade unionist. His agenda in early years included a trade union confederation of Scheduled Castes, Scheduled Tribes and Backward Caste (reference was to non-Dalit castes, who were economically backward). A fiery speaker, Kanshi Ram urged all non-upper castes to unite under the leadership of the BSP. He was unable to form this larger united front, but very successful in organising *Dalits* under the banner of his party. It was a huge setback for the Congress Party because it relied on *Dalit*-Muslim vote bank in North India for its electoral strategy. The BSP has had a great success in the largest province- U.P. (Uttar Pradesh) - Under the leadership of Kanshi Ram's protégé, Mayawati. In Punjab, however, the party's success has come only from an alliance with other parties. In electoral alliance with the Akali Dal, whom the Dalit leaders had always condemned as party of the upper-caste landlords, BSP won three parliamentary seats in 1996, including Kanshi Ram's seat from Hoshiarpur. On its own, the BSP was only successful in winning 9 seats in an assembly of 117 in 1992, when the Akali Dal had boycotted the elections under threat from Sikh terrorists. Less than a quarter of the eligible voters turned out to vote in the 1992 election, and the BSP was able to secure 16 per cent share of the popular vote. In 1997 assembly elections, the BSP managed to get one MLA elected with a 7.5 per cent share of the popular vote. In 2002 and 2007, the BSP drew blank as its popular vote share continued to decline to 5.7 per cent and 4.13 per cent respectively[16].

Despite the low levels of electoral support, the BSP has continued to enjoy a solid support of a sizeable number of loyal followers among *Dalits* in Punjab. Its leadership resented the domination of the upper castes in other parties. While the Congress for a long period of time continued to enjoy support among *Dalit* voters, the *Harijan* and *Balmiki* leaders remained only subordinates to the upper caste Congress leaders. The story was the same with other parties. This caste conscience had brought Prem Lal to the fold of BSP. A son of a *Dalit* Peon to an SDM (Sub-District Magistrate), Prem Lal was raised in an urban environment. It was a time when government officers were relatively honest and briberies existed only among the lowest echelons of bureaucracy. Prem Lal's father managed to make enough cash in addition to his meagre salary to educate his seven children, albeit only in government schools and colleges. The second youngest among his siblings, Prem Lal was the only child to become an officer in the family. He was not the brightest student, but thanks to India's reservation quota system for Dalits, Prem Lal got appointed as a *Naib Tehsildar*. He moved up the chain of command relatively quickly. He was also lucky to hold some crucial appointments at the levels of SDM and DTO (District Transport Officer). Times had changed; now the officers of Indian bureaucracy were more corrupt than any other strata of the administration. Prem Lal managed to accumulate huge amounts of ill-gotten wealth. Apart from the family's luxurious life-style, he was able to help his siblings except his elder sister who had married against her parents' wishes to a *Balmiki* Dalit. All four children of Prem Lal attended private English medium schools in a major metropolitan city. His eldest daughter moved to Germany with her IT graduate husband. Both his engineer sons became officers in state bureaucracy, one as an SDO (Sub-Division Officer) in PWD (Public Works Department), and the other as a first class officer of PCS (Provincial Civil Service). Prem Lal's youngest daughter became a medical doctor and opened her own private hospital.

Despite personal and family success, Prem Lal remained a bitter man. He always sensed that officers of the higher castes discriminated against him and other *Dalit* officers. He had even adopted the last name of upper Caste-*Jatt* Sikhs, but it did not help him in the socialization process with fellow officers. Furthermore, he felt he was not given the coveted position of a DC (Deputy Commissioner) of a district, although he held an equivalent rank in the Punjab Warehousing Corporation. The British had divided India into district level administrative units, each headed by an officer of Indian Civil Service. These officers, simply known as Collectors, were virtual Kings of each district. Under the command of provincial governors, they held the entire civil and police machinery of the district under their command. Independent India changed the name of this officer corps to IAS (Indian Administrative Service), but everything else remained British. Instead of colonial governors, the overall command passed into the hands of elected Chief Ministers of states. Although Punjab had 22 districts headed by a collector, Prem Lal's dream of becoming a DC remained unfulfilled. He blamed this on the upper caste Chief Ministers of Punjab. With the exception of Giani Zail Singh, a low caste *Tarkhan* (carpenter), all Chief Ministers of Punjab in independent India belonged to Hindu and Sikh upper castes. Since Chief Ministers made all administrative appointments and controlled all transfers, Prem Lal felt he was overlooked because of his Dalit caste.

The straw that finally broke the camel's back came at the time of his elder son's proposed marriage. Prem Lal's son fell in love with a *Brahmin* girl from the same colony. The girl's father was a junior officer in the department of statistics. The boy and girl wanted to marry each other with Prem Lal's blessings, but the girl's parents were adamantly opposed to such a union between a *Brahmin* woman and an untouchable man. They managed to register a number of cases against Prem Lal's son and other family members. Prem Lal felt that the district police chief, a *Jatt* Sikh, was more sympathetic to the Brahmin family than to his son. Despite his official position and other *Dalit* connections in higher echelons of power, Prem Lal was unable to move both the civil and police administration of the district because they openly sided with the woman's family. His son's final tactic to elope remained unfulfilled because the woman died under mysterious circumstances. Her funeral was over within hours of her death and to date no charges were brought against anyone by the police. After this, Prem Lal regularised his contacts with the BSP leadership and demanded a more active role. The party asked him to take early retirement from his government post and become a candidate for a parliamentary seat. He resigned but the seat was allocated to someone else who had close connections to UP Chief Minister Mayawati. Now, almost three years later, the BSP finally gave Prem Lal a seat. He knew he would not win, but, like many other candidates, it was a time to accumulate funds for the future.

Jagir Singh and Sarpanch were convinced that BSP candidate Prem Lal would be able to take a sizeable vote away from the Congress, and, as a result, it would be worth supporting his campaign. They discussed how vital financial resources could be directed to Prem Lal's campaign to ensure its smooth sailing. Changing topics, Jagir Singh inquired if liquor distribution among *Dalits* was satisfactory. *Sarpanch* was satisfied with the amount of liquor reaching *Dalit Mohallas*. However, he informed the Akali candidate that cheap whisky was fine for ordinary *Dalits*, but that higher quality liquor was required for *Dalit* leaders and those in higher echelons. Furthermore, *Sarpanch* asked if more rallies could be organized only with *Dalits*. As they were about to end the meeting, *Sarpanch* asked if arrangements were in order for Vitamin M. This was a code word for money to be distributed in cash to buy votes. "Don't worry, you will know everything," said Jagir Singh, as they were ending their meeting. "I have also inquired from a hospital in Delhi; they use foreign technology for knee operations," Jagir Singh assured *Sarpanch*. "We'll go there after the elections."

It was time for breakfast and Jagir Singh called his grandson, Ajay Pal Singh, to join. For any meeting over controversial issues, Jagir Singh had never invited a third person. He was no legal luminary, but he knew that if any substance of the meeting were to be leaked, it was safer if there were only two people. It will be 'your word and his word,' believed Jagir Singh. Although he was training his grandson to carry the family's legacy in politics, he did not want Ajay Pal Singh to attend the meeting with Sarpanch. A third person in a meeting, according to Jagir Singh, could be a potential witness. As Ajay Pal Singh walked in the room, Jagir Singh had a huge smile on his bearded face. He was disappointed in his three sons. They were unable to pursue the family legacy in politics. As a septuagenarian leader, Jagir Singh knew he needed to pass the torch. Now he was able to see the light at the end of the tunnel. Ajay Pal Singh finished his law degree and got elected to the Bar Association of Punjab and Haryana. He was also closer to the party leader's son. This gave a huge sigh of relief to Jagir Singh. He was now confident that his grandson had the potential to guard the family's political fiefdom for future generations. Politics, like caste, has become a dynastic trait in India.

References

1. For a general discussion of caste based on Vedas and Manu Smriti, see WM. Theodore De Bary (1958). *Sources of Indian Tradition.* (Volume I), New York: Columbia University Press.
2. For an extensive survey of the dominant castes, see Denzil Ibbetson (1987). *Punjab Castes: Races, Castes and Tribes of the Punjab.* Delhi:

Cosmo; and also H.A. Rose (1996). *Glossary of the Tribes and Castes of the Punjab and North West Frontier Province.* Delhi: Asian Educational Services.

3. Shinder Purewal (2000). *Sikh Ethno-nationalism and the Political Economy of Punjab.* New Delhi: Oxford University Press, pp. 4-5.

4. All 2007 data for caste vote is taken from a study published in EPW. See "Fourteenth Assembly Elections in Punjab" (2012). *Economic and Political Weekly*, Vol. 47 (14): 71-75.

5. In my conversations with candidates, MLAs and MPs from all different parties, a remarkable similar pattern of caste base voting behaviour has emerged. There are, of course, other variables, which include the region, size of each caste, strength of individual candidate in different sections of community, and wedge issues which emerge during campaigns. Otherwise mostly it's believed that *Jatt* Sikhs predominantly vote the Akali Dal, while the Congress is their second choice. Among the *Brahmins* and the *Kayasthas*, the first and second choices have shifted between the two main national parties: the Congress and the BJP. The inter-mediate castes present a unique phenomenon because they have numerical strength only in a very few constituencies. The main perspective on their voting behaviour is that they often tend to vote for their own community candidate if he/she is representing a major party; otherwise they are considered very strategic voters-voting for the winner. The *Dalit* voters have two major divisions: the *Balmiki* community tend to be divided between the Akali Dal and the Congress Party, and the *Harijans* are divided between the BSP and the Congress.

6. A constitutional amendment is required every ten years to keep this affirmative action program entrenched. No party or individual Member of Parliament has ever opposed this contitutional amendment. members of the top brass of the Dalit community, which benefits from this quota system, have built almost a religious   following among community members to ensure that no politician will ever dare to oppose these special privileges.

7. See Shinder Purewal (2011). Sikh Diaspora and the Movement for Khalistan. *Indian Journal of Political Science*, LXXII (4): 1131-1142.

8. *Indian Express*, August 16, 2010.

9. *The Tribune, February* 24, 2012.

10. A Jewish proverb.

11. An African proverb.

12. *Ibid.*

13. *Ibid*

14. *Indian Express*, March 29, 2012.
15. *Times of India*, January 23, 2012.
16. All election data is available from the website of Election Commission of India, http://ECI.NIC.in under the heading 'Past Elections'.

3

The Dynastic Politics

Man will never be free until the last king is strangled with the entrails of the last priest

– Denis Diderot

Jagir Singh's desire to pass the political baton to his grandson was not an isolated desire. The Indian political landscape has been filled with political dynasties. In 1947, the British left behind 565 princely states whose royal families had autonomous status within the Raj. Indra Gandhi's populist politics ended the perks and royal status of these dynastic rulers. 65 years after independence, however, democratic politics has established less than half that number of families in control of state and central legislatures. The most powerful and established dynasty has been the Nehru-Gandhi family. Since independence, the Nehru-Gandhi family has held power in Delhi for five decades, either directly from Jawaharlal Nehru to his daughter Indra Gandhi to her son Rajiv Gandhi, or indirectly through Dr. Manmohan Singh controlled by Rajiv's Italian Catholic wife Sonia Gandhi. The Nehru-Gandhi family's political legacy has been entrenched in the rich history of the Indian National Congress, the Grand Old Party (GOP) of Indian politics. Founded by a retired British civil servant Allan Hume in 1885 to give voice to Indians in the British Raj, the Congress ultimately became a united front for all nationalist forces of India. Initially it remained a small elitist organisation, but the entry of Mahatma Gandhi after the World War I changed the fortunes of the Congress. It became a mass organisation under the leadership of Mahatma. The Nehru family's participation in the Congress, however, had started with Motilal Nehru who served two-terms as its President. The legacy was carried by his son, Jawaharlal Nehru. A Fabian socialist, Jawaharlal Nehru led the left wing of the Congress party. He became a close confidant of Mahatma Gandhi. As a result, the Congress elected Nehru to be the Prime Minister of newly independent India after the partition of the sub-continent in 1947. Although a dominant personality in both the Congress and the government, Nehru had to share power with many other great leaders of the party, including Sardar Patel.

When Nehru died in May 1964, he was succeeded by Lal Bahadur Shastri. Apparently the Congress president Kamraj initially offered the post to Nehru's daughter, Indra Gandhi[1], but she declined. The actual struggle for power was between the left-wing of the Congress led by Shastri and the right-wing led by Morarji Desai. As the dominant group, the left-wing, with the help of Indra Gandhi, succeeded in defeating the followers of Desai. Unfortunately, Shastri died soon after signing the Tashkent agreement to settle the 1965 war with Pakistan in January, 1966. The left-right struggle soon erupted in the ranks of the Congress party, but Indra Gandhi won the power struggle with relative ease. She became India's third Prime Minister in 1966. As she tried to subdue and expel her opponents from the Congress ranks, a culture of sycophancy developed in the once mighty GOP of Indian politics. In her attempts to pursue populist left wing politics, she had to sideline various regional agrarian leaders. As a result, she devised a policy of mobilising Muslims and *Dalits* under the leadership of upper castes to boost the Congress ranks[2]. She started running the Congress in the style of the *Mughal* rule. In order to minimize revolts against their rule, the *Mughals* did not allow any revenue officials to own land, and the positions of these officials were not hereditary. The temporary nature of their positions made them loyal to the *Mughal* rulers and, hence, unable to organise or support any uprisings.

Indra Gandhi eliminated powerful state leaders and promoted sycophants who had no political base. This same policy has remained central to the Congress organisation at present. Mrs. Gandhi did, however, firmly entrench the almighty role of the Nehru-Gandhi family in the party. Although players changed to a certain degree, the loyalty continued during the rule of her son, Rajiv Gandhi, when he became the 6th Prime Minister of India. In fact, Indra Gandhi was raising her younger son, Sanjay Gandhi, to be her political heir but he died in a plane crash. The quiet pilot of Indian Airlines, Rajiv Gandhi was brought into the sphere of politics after this tragedy. The politics of assassination took the lives of both Indra Gandhi, murdered by her Sikh bodyguards in 1984, and Rajiv Gandhi, murdered by Tamil secessionists during an election campaign rally in 1991. More than three decades of almost monopolistic Congress rule under the Nehru-Gandhi family rule had established a huge network of 'honorary Gandhis'[3] in all states and union territories of India. Most of these loyalists owed their positions in the party, government, bureaucracy, business, and civil society to the blessings of the Nehru-Gandhi family. Although the Congress party decided to go with the leadership of Prime Minister Narsimha Rao after Rajiv Gandhi's assassination, the honorary Gandhis never abandoned their struggle to bring the power back to the fold of the Nehru-Gandhi family. They finally succeeded to recruit Rajiv Gandhi's widow, Sonia Gandhi, who was reluctant to enter the domain of politics. She became the Congress President and led a successful campaign in 2004, defeating the government of the BJP. As she was slated to become India's Prime Minister, the opposition launched an agitation against a 'foreigner' holding such high office. The Indian constitution did not bar any foreign born person to hold any constitutional office, but the defeated opposition found an emotional issue to corner her. However, she proposed the name of the former finance minister, Dr. Manmohan Singh, for the post of the Prime Minister and silenced her critics. As this was a Congress led coalition government, Sonia Gandhi got elected as Chairperson of this UPA (United Progresive Allaince). This position has allowed her control of the Prime Minister's Office as well as the entire cabinet. Now, the family's next move would be to prepare Rajiv-Sonia's son, Rahul Gandhi, to take over the Party and the government.

In Punjab, the politics at state levels has been dominated by 6 wealthy *Jatt* Sikh families: the *Maharaja* of Patiala family, the Badal family of Muktsar, the Majithia family of Amritsar, the Kairon family of Taran Tarn, the Brar family of Sarai Nagra and the Mann family of Sangrur[4]. A journalist from *India Today* noted that through inter-clan marriages these families have created a political heaven "that ensures that no family is ever completely out of power"[5] regardless of which party controlled the executive power. The Congress leadership has been in the hands of its president and former Chief Minister, Captain Amarinder Singh, a *Jatt* Sikh of Sidhu sub-caste and a scion of royal family from the former princely state of Patiala. The Gandhi family has not allowed any one Congress family to emerge as the dominant center of power in the state. Captain Amarinder Singh, however, was an exception. Although his power has been seriously checked by the distribution of key positions to his arch-rivals in both the party and the Congress governments at both Center and state, he has survived even with an open challenge to his party leadership's position vis-à-vis the distribution of river waters of Punjab. This former officer of the Indian army was brought to the fold of the Congress by Rajiv Gandhi. He entered the *Lok Sabha* (lower house of Indian Parliament) in 1980, but resigned from the Congress caucus in protest against the Indian Army's entry in the Golden Temple, the holiest shrine of Sikhism in Amritsar. After this rebellion, he not only joined the Congress party's chief rival, the Akali Dal, but also founded his own Akali Dal-*Panthic*- as he parted company with other Akali leaders. However, he was quick to re-join the Congress as Sonia Gandhi became its President. She named him the president of the Punjab Congress and became its Chief Minister in 2002, after defeating his old Akali comrades. As Chief Minister, he openly defied the Congress high command over the issue of water sharing with the neighbouring state of Patiala. The Congress under the Gandhis has never allowed such deviance but Amarinder Singh had a very unique status as an honorary Gandhi. First and foremost, he has a historical base as a member of the royal family of Patiala. Thus, even without executive power, he enjoyed certain authority based on tradition[6]. Secondly, he was a classmate and a friend of Rajiv Gandhi at Doon school, India's Eaton. The legend has it that he also played a role in Rajiv Gandhi's marriage to Sonia Maino. As a result, both families have maintained a strong social bond. Whether the Captain would be able to establish a democratic dynasty has yet to be seen. His wife, Praneet Kaur, has been serving as a minister of state for external affairs in the UPA government since 2009, and his son, Raninder Singh, was nominated as a candidate for the Punjab Assembly. The Captain's mother, Mohinder Kaur, was an elected Member of Parliament from Patiala, and his father, Yadvinder Singh, had close personal relations with Prime Minister Nehru.

While the Nehru-Gandhi family has not allowed the establishment of one powerful Congress family in any state, the family has tolerated dynasties of honorary Gandhis at local levels for both assembly and parliamentary constituencies. The permission has been based on two conditions: (i) the local honorary Gandhis must remain loyal to the Nehru-Gandhi family, and (ii) they must be able to win seats for the Congress. In swing ridings, the local Congress dynasties have always lived on a cliff. In Dholpur, the Congress candidate Amar Singh was in this dangerous position. In this election, the risk was even greater because the assembly elections were being held in the newly demarcated constituencies. The old base of most MLA's had disappeared and new areas from neighbouring constituencies had been added. A defeat would be a second strike because Amar Singh had lost to the Akali Dal's Jagir

Singh in 2007. Two consecutive losses in assembly elections could endanger anyone's candidacy. Although he was in the third generation of the honorary Gandhis, the position came with strings attached. Amar Singh's family dynasty in politics was started by his grandfather, Sardar Tej Singh. Hailing from a humble background, Tej Singh joined the British Indian army before World War I. British preference for *Jatt* Sikhs in Punjab made it relatively easy for Taj Singh to join the ranks of an infantry battalion, which was stationed in Iraq during the War. Although soldiers showed great loyalty to the British Empire, the racial discrimination by white officers and nationalist propaganda also made them conscience of India's struggle for independence. Tej Singh was one of those who joined anti-British agitations immediately after retirement. He first joined the *Gurdwara Sudar Lehar* (Sikh Temple Reform Movement) in the ranks of the Akali Dal. Most historic Sikh temples were occupied by corrupt pro-British priests. In the 1920s, a movement started to liberate those temples. As a result, two important institutions of Sikh politics were born: (i) the Akali Dal, a political party of the Sikhs, and (ii) the *Sharomani Gurdwara Prabandhik* Committee (SGPC-Management Committee to control historic Sikh Temples).

As usual, the British threw many protesters in jail. It was in jail that Tej Singh's life took a different turn. He met a Congress leader in jail who became his Guru. Impressed with his Guru's wisdom and advice, Tej Singh remained a loyal disciple to his mentor for the rest of his life. The urban educated Hindu nationalist Guru had great knowledge and respect for Sikh traditions. Tej Singh became almost like an adopted son seeking advice from this wise man on every aspect of life. It never failed as Tej Singh started moving up in the ranks of the Congress. In financial terms, he started taking an interest in trade and commerce. On the advice of his Congress Guru, he also shifted his children to well managed urban schools. After independence in 1947, Tej Singh became a major power bloc in local politics. With the help of his mentor, who was now a state cabinet minister, Tej Singh did not have any trouble in expanding his business, as licenses and permits were obtained without much hassle with bureaucracy. In the 1951 elections, he was hopeful for a party nomination from Dholpur, but another powerful leader belonging to a different faction managed to sideline Tej Singh. Although many supporters suggested him to declare his candidacy as an Independent, he remained loyal to the Congress on the advice of his mentor. By the time of the 1957 assembly election, Tej Singh had become a more powerful leader because the sitting candidate lost his position in factional feuds of the Congress Party's state unit. By now, Tej Singh was also a major transporter of the region. His trucking company controlled most of the transport business in his district along with the trade of opium and poppy husk.

The assembly elections of 1957 were a cake-walk for the Congress because it fielded candidates in alliance with the Akali Dal. The main opposition came from the CPI (Communist Party of India), which had led an agitation of peasants and farm workers in the state. The CPI managed to get nearly 14 per cent of the popular vote in this election- its highest ever in Punjab[7]. Tej Singh not only won this election, but was victorious in 1962 and 1967, after the second partition of Punjab. The British Punjab was a huge province with areas of current Pakistani Punjab and Islamabad in addition to Indian states of Punjab, Haryana, Himachal Pradesh and the Union Territory of Chandigarh. The 1931 religious census records showed that Punjab had 56 per cent Muslims, 30 per cent Hindus and only 13 per cent Sikhs. In 1947, in the largest migration of humans in the 20th century, almost the entire Muslim population shifted to West Pakistan while Hindus and Sikhs came to settle in Indian Punjab. In Indian Punjab, the Hindus became a new majority with 62 per cent of the population compared with 35 per cent Sikhs[8]. The Sikh leadership was interested in a province with a Sikh majority- hence the Akali agitation for a new language based province. In 1966, the demand was met and a new Punjabi *suba* (state) was carved, which gave the Sikhs a majority status with 60 per cent of the state's population compared with 35 per cent Hindus. Although Tej Singh won his constituency in 1967, the Congress lost power. In this new Sikh-dominated Punjab, the Akali Dal became a formidable opponent. Two Akali governments under the Chief Ministership of Justice Gurnam Singh, a *Jatt* Sikh of Grewal sub-caste, and Lachman Singh, a *Jatt* Sikh of Gill sub-caste, collapsed in as many years. Now Tej Singh was trying to pass the family's political legacy to his younger son, Partap Singh, because his elder son was more interested in business and alcohol. As a result of a mid-term poll, he had no option but to be a candidate in the 1969 election. Once again, the Congress lost the battle of the ballot in new Punjab, and, along with Congress, Tej Singh lost his own seat. A new rival, Jagir Singh, a *Jatt* Sikh, won the constituency for the Akali Dal.

Fortunes changed in 1972; after India's successful intervention in the Bangladesh war, Indra Gandhi became goddess Durga. The Congress swept all parliamentary and assembly polls and Tej Singh was able to nominate his son Partap Singh who won Dholpur constituency back from Jagir Singh. Like his father, Partap Singh was unable to secure a cabinet position in the Congress government in Chandigarh. After the emergency period of 1975 to 1977, when all civil liberties were suspended by Indra Gandhi, the Congress lost ground to its electoral rivals. A coalition of left, right, and center parties led by the Akali Dal defeated the Congress in 1977 assembly elections in Punjab. Although Congress had secured a bigger share of the popular vote, a coalition of the Akali Dal, Janata Party, and the Communists managed to secure more seats. This strange alliance had its inherent contradictions, but the bigger challenge came from the emergence of Sikh militancy and the demand for a separate Sikh state in 1978. A similar strange alliance under the banner of the Janata Party had also come to power in Delhi under the leadership of Mrs. Gandhi's old rival, Morarji Desai. This first non-Congress government in Delhi collapsed and new elections brought Indra Gandhi's Congress back to power in 1980. Immediately after her return to power, Mrs. Gandhi put an end to the Akali government as the 'law and order' situation deteriorated in Punjab. Fresh assembly elections in 1980 brought the Congress back to power under the Chief Ministership of Darbara Singh, a *Jatt* Sikh of Johal sub-caste.

The decade of the 1980s witnessed an abnormal period for democratic politics in Punjab. State governments were dismissed in favour of the President's rule in the face of a deteriorating law and order situation. Normally Indra Gandhi was known for her distaste of opposition led governments in the states, but now she was even forced to dismiss a Congress government in Punjab. As terrorist violence escalated after the Indian Army's entry in the Golden Temple and organized massacres of Sikhs after Mrs. Gandhi's assassination, some Sikh politicians decided to leave the ranks of the Congress. Partap Singh, and his family, however, remained ever so loyal to the Nehru-Gandhi family thus earning a special place in the ranks of the honorary Gandhis. In 1985, once again Partap Singh raised the Congress banner as a candidate in Dholpur, but lost to a new young Akali candidate because Jagir Singh refused candidacy on the advice of his factional leader, Parkash Singh Badal. The Congress received nearly 40 per cent of the popular vote compared with Akali Dal's 38 per cent, but the first-past-the-post electoral system did not favour the Congress seat tally. The Akali Dal formed a majority government under Surjit Singh Barnala's leadership with 73 seats compared with only 32 for the Congress. Elections were called after the new Prime Minister had signed a major political settlement with the Akali Dal President, Sant Harchand Singh Longowal- popularly known as the Rajiv-

Longowal Agreement. The agreement was never implemented and the
terrorists assassinated Longowal for signing a document with the Indian
government. The new government did not last long as the President's
rule was imposed on Punjab. Partap Singh had to wait until 1992 for new
assembly elections in Punjab. As the Akali Dal boycotted this election
under Sikh terrorist threats, the Congress had a plain field. Unfortunately
the day Partap Singh was announced as a candidate from Dholpur by the
Congress, he was killed by terrorist bullets. Before he died in hospital,
he appointed his son Amar Singh as his successor and requested that the
party nomination should go to him. The party was also keen on fielding a
candidate from a 'martyr's' family.

Amar Singh was the middle child in a family of 7 siblings, three
brothers, and four sisters. All his sisters were college educated and
married to civil and army officers. Both of his younger brothers became
officers in para-military forces. Educated in an elite school of Himachal
Pradesh, Amar Singh could not finish his undergraduate studies. Despite
terrorist threats, however, he remained active in the ranks of the Congress
affiliated NSUI (National Student Union of India). In addition to serving
in the ranks of the Congress *Lok Seva Dal* (Social Service Agency), he
played a leading role in the Youth Congress as its executive member.
Faced with both verbal and physical attacks from the Congress Party's
opposition camps and the rival Congress factions, Amar Singh developed
a thick skin at an early age. As he believed in the principle of 'kill one
to warn a hundred'[9], he accumulated a lengthy criminal record from
charges of kidnapping to attempted murder. Thanks to the slow wheels of
Indian judiciary, some of the charges were still pending in higher courts
of appeal after two decades. He had told his friends that his childhood
dream was to become an army officer. He obviously did not succeed in
that dream, but he got married to a Colonel's daughter. His father used
to say that no girl could ever tolerate Amar Singh's lifestyle as a wife.
Whether it was Colonel's well known shooting skills, or the beauty of his
wife, Neelam, Amar Singh became a faithful husband. Although his wife
became pregnant five times, he only has two sons, both born after his first
electoral victory.

Under terrorist threat, only 23.82 per cent of the registered voters
turned out to vote in 1992. Most of this vote was in the urban areas. Amar
Singh won his first election without much competition. Unlike his father
and grandfather, he succeeded in securing a cabinet birth in the Congress
government. The newly formed government succeeded in restoring
normalcy in Punjab by the end of 1993, a decade and a half after the first

skirmishes in Amritsar in 1978. The man who brought peace to Punjab, Chief Minister Sardar Beant Singh, was assassinated by the terrorist of the Babar Khalsa group. The untimely murder of Beant Singh led to the infighting within the ranks of the Congress caucus for a successor. The Party decided to appoint Harcharn Singh Brar. The Congress finished the rest of the term rejoicing victory over terrorism and pursued no development work. As a result, the Congress lost the next election to the Akali Dal in 1997 with the lowest level of popular support in the history of electoral politics of post-1947 Punjab. It received only 26.59 per cent of the popular vote compared with the Akali Dal's 37.64 per cent[10]. Amar Singh lost the Dholpur seat to Jagir Singh. The wave of corruption that had reached new heights under the previous Congress government continued under the Chief Ministership of Parkash Singh Badal because most Akali ministers and legislatures had not had a chance to make money from public coffers in the past two decades. Although Akali Dal had formed a government in 1985, the loyalists of the Badal group had stayed away from Barnala's cabinet.

The tradition of anti-incumbency continued in Punjab during the 2002 assembly elections with the Congress victory under Captain Amarinder Singh. Amar Singh won the Dholpur seat back from Jagir Singh and once again landed a lucrative portfolio in the new cabinet. He had become wiser and more experienced. Loss teaches more important lessons than victory. He also learned that perception was everything in politics, thus he started making efforts to appear humble and honest. At the same time, he realized that compared with the un-competitive election of 1992, the role of money had grown substantially. With single-minded devotion, he was now focused on accumulating wealth. He knew that 'if you have money, people think you are wise, handsome, and able to sing like a bird'[11]. But history was not kind to Amar Singh and the Congress. The Akali Dal returned to power in 2007 as Punjab recorded one of the highest polling with more than 75 per cent of the eligible voters exercising their right to vote a decade and half after it had recorded the lowest polling with a less than one-quarter turn-out rate. If history was on their side, the Congress would be victorious in 2012. Amar Singh also needed to secure this seat for the Congress; otherwise, the dynastic rule was in danger.

The Congress has not been alone in pursuing dynastic politics. All other parties, with the exception of the BJP and Communist Parties (CPI and CPM), have developed their own 'royal' families. The Akali monarchy was now firmly entrenched in the Badal family. Chief Minister Parkash Singh Badal, a *Jatt* Sikh of Dhillon sub-caste, won his first seat in the Punjab legislature in 1957 when the Akali Dal fielded candidates in alliance with the Congress. A graduate of Forman Christian College, Lahore, he has established a clear and unchallenged leadership over a party known throughout its history for factionalism and feudal fights. His son, Sukhbir Singh Badal, has been appointed as the deputy Chief Minister of the state and the President of the Akali Dal. Several other members of his family have held various elected and appointed positions in both the state and central governments. Among them his nephew, Manpreet Singh Badal, his son-in-law Adesh Partap Singh Kairon, the brother-in-law of his son, Bikramjit Singh Majithia, as cabinet ministers, and his daughter-in-law, Harsimrat Kaur Badal, as a Member of Parliament. Another cabinet minister, Janmeja Singh Sekhon, was a close relative of the Badals. In a constitutionally mandated limit of 18 cabinet members, 6 members belonged directly to Chief Minister Badal's family and relatives. Through inter-clan marriage network, the Badals have established relations with all six powerful families of the state. Badal's son-in-law, Adesh Partap, is the grandson of the former Congress Chief Minister Partap Singh Kairon. Partap Singh Kairon's niece was married to Harcharan Singh Brar, who became the Congress Chief Minister of Punjab after Beant Singh's assassination. Deputy Chief Minister Sukhbir Badal's wife, Harsimrat Kaur, and his brother-in-law, Bikramjit Singh Majithia, are grandchildren of Sardar Surjit Singh Majithia who served as India's deputy defence minister in Prime Minister Nehru's Congress government. Bikram Singh Majhithia's cousin is married to Capt. Amarinder Singh's daughter Jaya. Captain Amarinder Singh and Sharomani Akali Dal (Amritsar) leader, Simaranjit Singh Mann, are brothers-in-law, as their wives are sisters[12].

The story of the Badal family's total control of Akali Dal has been nothing short of a miracle. The party came out of a mass movement of the 1920's to liberate Sikh historic temples from corrupt priests. In response to this party's demands, the British passed the *Gurdwara* Act in 1925, which created the SGPC. At a time of limited franchise based on property and educational requirements, the *Gurdwara* Act gave every Sikh adult over the age of 21 the right to vote to elect SGPC members. The Akali Dal continued to participate in the nationalist struggle led by the Congress Party under the leadership of Mahatma Gandhi. Most of the Akali leaders in the early period of its existence came from urban *Kayastha* Sikh families. At the time of partition and immediately thereafter, the majority of its leaders thought the existence of Akali Dal in independent India was superfluous. However, two cardinal issues for

Sikhs revived the fortunes of the Akali party- the first issue was that of the Punjabi language in the 1951 census, and the second issue was related to the linguistic division of Punjab. The British had organized provinces more for the convenience of administration, not taking into account the history, culture, and language of those regions. The Congress, however, had promised to create new provinces based on the 'language formula.' The Sikh leaders, who found themselves in a new minority in the Punjab, started demanding the division of the state on the basis of Punjabi language. In order to deny this legitimate demand of a linguistic state, the Hindu leadership urged all Punjabi Hindus to register their mother tongue as Hindi in the 1951 census. Although this report on language affiliation was never released by Census India, it was commonly believed that the majority of Hindus had reported their mother tongue as Hindi. *Rig Veda*, the oldest living written document in the world, was written in the land of Punjab. In addition, many other religious books of Hinduism were also written in this land of five rivers. In fact, the Punjabi language was created by Hindus. They had developed Punjabi language centuries before the Muslims started arriving in Punjab and certainly long before Sikhism was even born. It was a strange decision of Hindu leadership to break a historic link with its own mother tongue. Fortunately, no other Hindu community in other parts of India ever reached such irrational conclusions.

Although various excuses were invented not to bi-furcate the state of Punjab on the basis of language formula, the central government finally made a decision after the Indo-Pak war of 1965, in which the Sikh soldiers played a valiant role, to create a Punjabi *Suba* (state). In the new Sikh majority state, the electoral fortunes of Akali Dal witnessed a new dawn. In fact, the party formed the first two governments after linguistic partition, albeit both minority coalitions. Parkash Singh Badal took over the reins of power as Chief Minister in Akali Dal's second victory in 1969 in alliance with *Jan Sangh*, the predecessor of the BJP. It was not an easy task to take over the leadership of the party of local-independent warlords. The Akali *Jathedars* (local leaders) had remained fiercely independent under all previous party leaders. Once at the party's helm, Badal started limiting the powers of the *Jathedars* and eliminating the power of his rivals. He certainly believed that there were only 2 perfect rivals- 'one dead and the other unborn'[13]. It took him nearly 4 decades to complete the process, but finally he has emerged not only the sole unchallenged leader of the party but also in a position to pass on his political legacy to his son, Sukhbir Singh Badal. Comparing his leadership to the historic figure of Maharaja Ranjit Singh, Badal's biographers have paraphrased Warren Hastings:

"The Sikhs, so eminently suited to the military profession, could not become very powerful because of their spirit of independence and frequent internal warfare but they were prompt to rally together at the call of a common danger."[14]

History tells us that Sikhs were never 'prompt' to form unity in the face of any danger. Despite Afghan invasions, the Sikh *Misls* (military formations) under the command of various leaders refused to join hands; and in fact, they were often united with the enemy against each other. It took the military might of Maharaja Ranjit Singh, a *Jatt* Sikh warrior, to eliminate the power of other *Misls* and put an end to Afghan invasions. After more than a thousand years of Islamic invasions, Maharaja Ranjit Singh had established the first Punjabi Kingdom in 1799, which lasted till the end of the Anglo-Sikh wars in 1849. He would have been unable to secure his leadership without the forceful elimination of other Sikh warlords. In a similar fashion, the Akali leaders were never able to form unity even at a time when Sikhs were being massacred in Delhi and other places in the wake of Mrs. Gandhi's assassination. It took the Machiavellian manoeuvers of Parkash Singh Badal to eliminate the modern warlords of Akali politics to establish his hegemony. As a result, loyalty to the Badal family has become now the sole criterion to join the ranks of Akali legislators and other ranks within the party.

Jagir Singh was one of those loyal soldiers of Badal dynasty. His father, Rai Bahadur Sardar Nihal Singh Randhawa, was a local leader of the Unionist Party of Punjab. The Unionist Party was a secular alliance of Punjabi landlords fiercely loyal to the British rule. Under the charismatic leadership of Sir Sikander Hayat Khan, one of the biggest Muslim landlords of western Punjab, the Unionist Party dominated the provincial legislature between both World Wars. Among Hindu and Sikh landlords, Sir Khan was supported by his loyal lieutenants, Sir Chotu Ram and Sir Sunder Singh Majhithia respectively. Although Muslims were a majority in Punjab, the right to vote was based on property and educational qualifications. In this respect, the Sikhs and Hindus formed the majority of the vote bank of Punjab. Thus, local Sikh landlords like Nihal Singh with the right to vote were important pillars of the Unionist Party. The party was vigorously opposed to the Congress declaration for complete independence for India. For Nihal Singh, who was also a British spy, it was a dangerous declaration. Through his extensive network, Nihal Singh had provided vital information to authorities on the activities of revolutionaries and other anti-British forces. For this service, he was targeted by the patriotic forces, but awarded with the title of 'Rai Bahadur' by the Crown. The British also gave him several hectares of revenue free land.

After World War II, the British decided to leave India. It came as a shock to people like Nihal Singh. Soon after independence, however, Nihal Singh realized that nothing had changed for the family and its status. As rich landlords, they became the center of attention for politicians and government officials. In the post-independence period, local power blocs became important pillars of patronage distribution networks. Nihal Singh was never interested in entering electoral contests, asking for votes with folded hands from ordinary people was simply beneath his privileged status. However, he had developed important links with political figures of the new Punjab. He married his elder son, Jagir Singh, to the daughter of an Akali leader, who had served as an important member of the SGPC. This connection was crucial for Jagir Singh's entry in the Akali Dal. Jagir Singh started participating in Punjabi *suba* agitation of the party and got arrested on two occasions. For Akali activists, political arrests on the resume were crucial to advance through the ranks. After losing the local constituency in the 1967 election, the Akali leadership was searching for a winning candidate in Dholpur. Thanks to his father-in-law's connections, Jagir Singh got the party's nod in 1969 and won his seat. In this minority Akali government led by Parkash Singh Badal, Jagir Singh developed a loyal relationship with the Chief Minister. Subsequently, he won this seat in 1977, 1997, and 2007. Although the constituency area had changed under the new demarcation of boundaries act, Jagir Singh was hopeful and praying for a win.

Jagir Singh was unable to pass the legacy to his sons, as they had shown no signs of political inclination. His grandson, however, had chosen the 'right path'. Educated and smart, Ajay Pal Singh had aligned himself with the future of the party- Sukhbir Singh Badal. Sukhbir Badal has shown to his father that he had superb organisational skills. The 'old' Akali Dal had suffered from a generation gap with older leaders controlling the party while student and youth leaders were drifting to emotional appeals of militant-fundamentalist forces within the Sikh community. The Congress, in particular, had used this rift for its strategic advantages in electoral politics. Sukhbir Badal's ability to directly control both the student and youth wings has denied the Congress the services of the 'fifth column.' He has already taken over the party's presidency, and, in dynastic politics, he would follow his father as the Chief Executive of the state. For Jagir Singh, the victory in this election would consolidate the family's hold on local power through Sukhbir Badal's protégé, and his grandson-Ajay Pal Singh. Jagir Singh, however, knew not to 'bargain for fish which were still in the water'[15]. His greatest worry was Sukhbir Badal's policy, like his father, to keep a number of loyalists competing in every constituency.

While the gatekeepers of the old established and successful parties have been guarding their entrenched positions, democracy has a way of opening doors to new comers. Third parties with less success in the electoral field and the arrival of new parties in political domain have created more room for new aspirants. In Punjab, the emergence of the PPP (People's Party of Punjab) had opened the gates for aspiring politicians like its candidate from Dholpur, Ashok Kumar Garg, a *Bania* (moneylender) by caste. Garg's parents and grandparents were involved in the old family business of lending money and running retail shops in a small town. A graduate with an MBA, he took the family business in a more profitable direction. He started a new venture in modern banking with an NRI partner from the United States. This foreign connection was crucial not only for attracting NRI accounts but also in money laundering operations. The business grew at the speed of light and they now had 78 branches in seven districts of Punjab. According to his college friends, Garg had shown no interest in any business ventures during his student days. He was a Bollywood fan, and wanted to marry a woman like Hema Malini (a Bollywood star of similar status to Elizabeth Taylor). As a student union activist, he dreamed about public office. He was short and unattractive, but wealth and the arranged marriage system fulfilled his first desire. Now he had a beautiful wife and two sons, both ugly like their father.

Garg contributed liberally to the Congress coffers during the provincial and federal elections. Despite all this wealth, he was unable to secure even an appointed position at state level when the party was in power. Disappointed in the Congress, he turned his attention to the BJP. The Kayastha and Brahmin dominated leadership in the area had no room for this swinging Bania but he found a new hope. The Akali Dal under Sukhbir Badal started turning its attention to accommodating the Hindu community in Punjab so as to expand its base in urban areas. The party, with its base in rural Punjab, has always relied on the BJP, with its base in urban centers, for electoral victories and formation of governments. In governance, both coalition partners have engaged in a tug-of-war to share development funds for their respective rural and urban bases. The Punjab unit of the BJP has been unable to expand its base in the rural region. Historically, the *Jan Sangh*, the predecessor of the BJP, was a party of urban shopkeepers, traders, and merchants. The new party in the form of the BJP has not been able to move beyond its old traditional base because its leadership base was still confined to shopkeepers, traders and merchants. Realising the inability of the BJP leadership to move beyond the urban regions, the Akali Dal had adopted a strategy to move in the urban centers. It had a better chance to succeed in urban Punjab because a sizeable population of upper caste Sikh *Kayastha* lived in the cities. In addition to this base, attracting Hindu politicians with a political base to the Akali Dal would eventually make the party more competitive in urban areas thus weakening their reliance on the BJP.

This strategy of Akali leadership had attracted the attention of many Hindu politicians, who could not find any accommodation in either the Congress or the BJP ranks. Garg also thought that finally his second wish from College days to hold public office would be realized. However, he was mistaken. As they say, 'an old patient is better than a new doctor'[16]. The Akali Dal decided to go with an established leader of Bania community in the constituency Garg had requested a nomination. Like many others who could not find accommodation in the ranks of three major political outfits in Punjab, Garg was looking for a chance in a new party. Luckily a new movement had emerged that formed a brand new party in the state-the People's Party of Punjab (PPP). Chief Minister Badal's nephew and the state's finance minister, Manpreet Singh Badal, had separated from his family's party, Akali Dal, in October 2010. At the time, the political circles were full of rumours that senior Badal would appoint his son, Sukhbir Badal, as his successor to the Chief Minister's throne. Manpreet Badal launched a pre-emptive strike by accusing his own government of destroying Punjab's economy and finances by pumping billions in state subsidies for farmers. As a rich landlord, Manpreet had also benefited from the same subsidies but leading by example was an alien concept in Punjab politics. State Chief Minister, Parkash Singh Badal, claimed that he had given everything his nephew ever wanted and the boy simply 'betrayed' him. However, the Chief Minister's younger brother, Gurdas Badal (Manpreet's father), argued that Parkash Singh Badal had reneged on his promise to make Manpreet his successor[17].

Once ousted from the party and the government, Manpreet Badal adopted an aggressive posture and launched 'a people's movement' to end corruption and nepotism from governance. Garg was quick to join this movement and became an early supporter with loads of money. The 'like-minded' populists decided to form a political party under the leadership of Manpreet Badal. In a massive gathering at Khatkar Kalan, the ancestral village of legendary Shaheed (martyr) Bhagat Singh, the new alliance of old and new leaders announced the formation of the PPP. Some of the biggest landlords, transporters and bankers had gathered on the stage to take an oath in front of the statue of a Marxist-Leninist nationalist. Had he been alive and governing India, Bhagat Singh would have appropriated the lands, properties, and wealth of all these multi-millionaires gathered on the stage. Manpreet Badal, however, found nothing strange in appropriating the revolutionary traditions of this popular historic figure. The mass euphoria that erupted after the founding of PPP lasted only a few months. Long before the election of 2012, it had become clear that the new party was destined for failure. Garg had already been campaigning, thus he had no choice but to carry the flag of the PPP in Dholpur. The sharp minds he had hired to run his campaign advised him to focus on a respectable showing by garnering a few thousand votes. The advice was based on the expectation that such a showing would strengthen his bargaining position with any party in the next election. Garg realized that apart from his regular campaign, the need of the hour was to seek the blessings of the local godman-*Baba-jee*. He had been a regular contributor to the donation box of *Baba-Jee*'s *Dera* (abode). The *Dera* had a large following among eligible voters who respected every command of *Baba-Jee*.

References

1.	Indra's Gandhi last name has nothing to do with great Mahatma. She was married to a Gujrati named Feroz Shah Gandhi; hence the epithet.

2.	Shinder Purewal (2000). *Sikh Ethnonationalism and the Political Economy of the Punjab*. Delhi: Oxford University Press, p. 101.

3.	The idea is taken from Thurston Clarke's use of the term 'honorary Kennedys' in his book *The Last Campaign: Robert F. Kennedy and 82 Days that Inspired America.* New York: Henry Holt & Company, 2008.

4.	*India Today*, January 14, 2012.

5.	*Ibid.*

6.	Traditional authority based on tradition (Max Weber).

7.	All election data is from the website of Election Commission of India (past elections): http://ECI.NIC.In

8.	J.S. Grewal (1996). *The Akalis: A Short History*. Chandigarh: Punjab Studies Publications, pp. 111-12.

9. A Chinese Proverb.
10. http://ECI.NIC.in. op. cit.
11. A Jewish proverb.
12. *India Today*, January 14, 2012.
13. The original Chinese proverb says 'there are two perfectly good men— one dead and the other unborn'.
14. S.R. Bakshi, Sita Ram Sharma and S. Gujrani (1998). *Contemporary Political Leadership of India: Parkash Singh Badal.* Delhi: APH Publishing, pp. 1-2.
15. An Indian proverb.
16. *Ibid.*
17. *India Today*, January 9, 2012.

4

The Godmen and Politicians:
An Unholy Alliance

*In all ages hypocrites, called priests, have put crowns upon the
leaders of the thieves, called Kings*
                                                        — Robert Green Ingersoll

In the land of 330 million gods and goddesses, there has never been
any dearth of holy men and women. Apart from the organized religious
traditions like Hinduism, Islam, Christianity, Judaism, Sikhism,
Buddhism, Jainism and others, one could literally witness millions of
holy men and women preaching and practicing spirituality in all parts
of India. From ancient times to date, these holy *Babas* have created
an independent space for themselves in the domain of spirituality.
Almost every village in India has a holy person apart from the priests of
organized religions. What set them apart from the organized ecclesiastical
authorities was often their secular nature catering to the spiritual needs
of people from all religious traditions and castes. In this tradition, Punjab
was no exception. While there had been tens of thousands of holy men
wandering around and settled in villages and towns of Punjab, a few have
emerged as powerful centers controlled by cult leaders-the Godmen.
People, especially from the lower castes and classes, dissatisfied with the
organized religious traditions of Hinduism and Sikhism rush to follow
these heterodox sects. Banerjee observes that:

> Sikh religious institutions have become identified with the
> powerful Jatt landlords....Those belonging to the lower castes
> in the community, and who are also the poorest, have been
> moving toward the reformist sects like the *Nirankaris* or the
> *Radhasoamis* which promise them a status of equality[1].

These heterodox sects not only attract the lower castes and poor from both Hinduism and Sikhism, they have also created a sense of belonging among their followers by making them part of these *Dera* communities. Democracy has always been a game of numbers, and hence these powerful centers of the Godmen have had attracted the attention of political candidates and political parties. Voting has been considered a psychological phenomenon, and campaigns have been aimed at controlling and altering the voters' state of mind. A voter's mind has few moments to reflect while standing in a polling booth exercising his or her choice in a secret ballot. Political leaders have known that the *Dera* cult leaders have the capacity to control the minds of the masses.

A huge controversy had erupted after the 2007 Punjab assembly elections when it was revealed that the *Dera Sacha Sauda* had issued an "open directive to its followers to vote for Congress....that made SAD (Sharomani Akali Dal-SP) lose Malwa."[2] This *Dera* headed by Baba Ram Rahim Singh was located in Sirsa, a town of Haryana bordering the Malwa region of Punjab. Since Malwa had most seats in the Punjab assembly (66 out of 117), the *Dera Sacha Sauda*'s move shook the Akali Dal. Despite loses in Malwa, the Akali Dal was able to form the government with its alliance partner the BJP largely as a result of its sweep in the Doaba and Majha regions with 25 and 26 seats in the Punjab assembly respectively. Unlike other *Dera*s, the *Sacha Sauda* has an open political wing that takes political decisions under the guidance of Baba Ram Rahim Singh. Ram Rahim has a very colourful past. A *Jatt* Sikh from the Ganganagar district of Rajasthan, he was a close associate of the Sikh militant, Gurjant Singh Rajasthani of the Khalistan Liberation Force (a terrorist outfit)[3]. In a favour to his close associate, Gurjant Singh killed the former chief of the *Dera Sacha Sauda*, Paran Pita Shah Satnam Singh Ji Maharaj thus clearing the way for Baba Ram Rahim Singh to succeed as *Dera* chief when he was only twenty three years old[4]. Ram Rahim has been accused of rape, murder, and possession of illegal arms[5], yet no political leader or party has raised even an eyebrow. Upset over his support to the Congress, however, the Akali Dal launched an agitation accusing Baba Ram Rahim of impersonating Guru Gobind Singh, the last Guru of the Sikhs. In a newspaper picture, Baba was shown dressed similarly to the portraits painted by modern artists of Guru Gobind. The Akali workers launched attacks on Dera Chief's followers, while its leadership made indoor deals with Baba Ram Rahim Singh. As a result, the *Dera Sacha Sauda* divided its support for both parties in two important parliamentary constituencies of Patiala and Bathinda in 2009. In Patiala, the *Dera* followers were asked to support Congress candidate Parneet Kaur, wife of Punjab Congress chief Captain Amarinder Singh, and in Bathinda, the *Premis* (as *Dera* followers are popularly known) were asked to back Harsimrat Kaur, daughter-in-law of Akali leader and Chief Minister Parkash Singh Badal[6].

Another politically important *Dera* has emerged in the Doaba region of Punjab. *Dera Sachkhand Balan* headed by Baba Niranjan Dass has been located in the Jalandhar district. This *Dera* has always been headed by a *Dalit*, and largely appeals to *Dalits* all over the Punjab. The region of Doaba has the highest concentration of the *Dalit* population in Punjab. Both democracy and the market-economy have made the upper echelons of *Dalits* important political and financial players of the region. A study pointed out that among the important and dominant business players in Jalandhar based leather and sports equipment industries were *Dalit* entrepreneurs[7]. Thus, the *Dera* Sachkhand's establishment and evolution in this important *Dalit* heartland has not been without logic. The *Dera*, however, has also attracted the wrath of the upper caste Sikh power blocs for its heterodox ways and attempts to move Sikh *Dalits* away from the mainstream Sikh community. In May 2009, its deputy chief, Sant Ramanand, was murdered by Sikh militants during his visit to Austria[8]. The controversy was centered on *Dera*'s attempts to create a new holy book by taking Bhagat Ravidas's compositions out of the Sikh holy book, *Guru Granth Sahib*. The Sikh holy book was unique among religious holy books. Compiled in 1604 by the fifth Guru, Arjan Dev, the *Guru Granth Sahib* included the compositions of various other Hindu saints and Muslim Sufis, apart from the compositions of five Sikh Gurus. Legend has it that Bhagat Ravidas, whose compositions were included in the Sikh holy book, belonged to the *Chamar* caste of the untouchables. Dera Sachkhand has created a new holy scripture called *Amritbani Guru Ravidas*, and declared this as the *Dalit* community's own holy book. Although this attempt to create a new *Dalit* identity has its religious base in the compositions of Guru Ravidas, the project was launched by the BSP chief Kanshi Ram in Varanasi in May, 1997. The foundation stone of Guru Ravidas Ghatt was laid in July, 1998, by the then *Dalit* President of India, K.R. Narayanan[9]. For electoral purposes, the BSP has lent full support to this *Dera*, but analysts believed that the *Dera* chiefs' main support was still going to the Congress. The BSP has only been the secondary beneficiary of electoral support from the *Dera* followers[10].

Another *Dera* with a large following not only in Punjab but also in other regions of North India has its main center situated in the border region of Majha. *Dera Radhasoami* of Beas has been headed by a *Jatt* Sikh, *Baba* Gurinder Singh Dhillon. The *Dera* has emerged as the biggest landlord in Punjab as it has *Satsang* (gathering of worshipers) grounds in most villages, towns, and cities of Punjab. Like many other *Deras*, the followers of *Radhasoami* also came mainly from *Dalits* and other lower castes and the poor. A well-organized corporate body of followers, the *Dera* has not created any open political controversies. In the past, however, it was an open secret that the *Dera* establishment was pro-Congress and most of the followers voted for the Congress. The politics of matrimonial connections has changed this perception. Bikram Singh Majhithia, brother-in-law of deputy chief minister and president of Akali Dal, Sukhbir Singh Badal, has married a close relative of the *Dera* Chief. Majhithia's wife, Ganeive Kaur Grewal, was a relative of *Baba* Gurinder Singh Dhillon. Did this mean that *Dera Radhasoami* would support Majhithia in his constituency or Akali Dal all over the state? There were, however, no indications that the *Dera*'s traditional practice of 'neutrality', or silent support for Congress, in politics would end anytime soon.

In the constituency of Dholpur, Garg knew very well that the larger *Dera*s would not ask their followers to support the candidates of minor third parties. Thus, he focused his attention on *Satya Dera* within the boundaries of the Dholpur constituency. Since he had donated a large amount of money to *Dera*'s various projects, Garg was hopeful that *Baba-Jee* would give him earthly blessings of votes. The sprawling *Dera* of *Baba-Jee* appeared more like a military station from outside with para-military soldiers guarding the gates and vicinity of this 'spiritual' center with machine-guns. Inside the four walls, one could experience life from a different planet. It was clean and organized with followers of *Baba-Jee* engaged in different activities in pure white clothes. The central *Kirtan* (singing of hymns) hall was half-covered and half-open to accommodate the *Sangat* (community of followers) in different climatic conditions. The *Dera* also had an elite English medium residential high school for boys and girls from rich families. Beside the school was a modern hospital which also granted nursing diplomas and degrees in association with a university in the United States. A large *Langar* (community kitchen) hall adjacent to the *Kirtan* Hall could feed hundreds of followers in one sitting. Three large guest houses accommodated followers from ordinary backgrounds, from the relatively wealthy upper castes, and those belonging to a VIP segment. A team of horticultural and agricultural experts have their own offices beside *Dera* security command center. This team has turned the *Dera* into a green estate with its own food and vegetable production. The most sacred place in this complex, however, was a very simple small brick room where devotees lined up to pay obeisance to the original founder of this *Dera-Satya Baba*.

Satya Baba was a simple wanderer from Rajasthan, well-known in the area for his expertise in traditional Indian medicine and for his spiritual nature. He would move from village to village to provide free medicine to the sick and to hold religious gatherings delivering the message of *Vedas* and *Guru Granth*. He neither believed in rituals, nor did he preach any. Along with medicine, he thought a spiritual message was vital in strengthening the resolve of a patient. Thus, he popularized Guru Nanak's message: *Man Jeete Jag Jeet* (he who conquered his mind has conquered the world). In the summer months, Satya Baba would travel north to the Himalayan hills along the banks of the river Ganga. During these journeys, he would exchange opinions with other holy men, collect plants for medicine, and meditate. Legend has it that Satya Baba cured a deadly disease of a local landlord and upon recovery this rich man gave ten acres of land to establish a *Dera* near his village. Although this wonderer never wanted to settle in one place, the new center started attracting people from distant places. It became more convenient to distribute medicine and spread spiritual message to people gathered in one place. His devotees were yearning to build a spacious palace type residence for him, but Satya Baba refused. Finally, he accepted a small and simple brick room, more out of his desire to keep medicine and holy books safe from adverse weather conditions, than personal comfort. He was more 'like a camel-carrying sweets but dining on thorns'[11].

The growing presence of this *Dera* not only attracted the faithful but also entrepreneurial minds and power blocs looking for socio-economic and political benefits from the 'spiritual wold.' Sher Singh Ahluwalia, a small retailer, was one of those cunning minds. Ahluwalia had known Satya Baba when he first began to visit the villages in this area. Initially Ahluwalia was after the secrets of *Baba*'s medicine to market these products, but after the establishment of the *Dera* he was able to imagine the larger picture. In the history of Punjab, the Ahluwalia caste has been relatively new to commerce and trade but very successful in this short period of time. Known as *Kalals*, they belonged to a very low caste of liquor producers in the countryside of Punjab. A new social movement of the *Khalsa* (baptized Sikhs) in eighteenth century Punjab provided them with an opportunity to advance their caste status. As the *Mughal* authority came under attack from various forces, especially the valiant Marathas, the *Khalsa* power blocs in Punjab organized several *Misls* (Military Formations). Since Sikhism allowed all castes to take baptism and join the order of the *Khalsa*, Jassa Singh Kalal of Alo Wal village became a *Khalsa* and organized a Sikh *Misil*. He added his village name as surname; hence the epithet Ahluwalia. The Ahluwalia *Misl* was eventually able to establish a small kingdom in Kapurthala. Although Maharaja Ranjit Singh eliminated the independence of all rival Sikh *Misls*, the Ahluwalia *Misl* survived in a subservient role under his mighty rule. Their efforts to join the ranks of warrior castes failed, but the community's long effort to follow the rites and rituals of *Kayastha* was successful. As a result, the Ahluwalia caste has now been claiming the status of the *Kayastha*[12].

Sher Singh Ahluwalia was the first among several entrepreneurial followers to suggest and establish a legal Trust to manage the *Dera*'s growing assets. Satya Baba had no interest in the Trust, but the trustees managed to buy new lands and expand the construction of new buildings. The families of trust members started witnessing a steady rise in their incomes and assets. These *nouveau* holy men attributed all this to the blessings of Satya Baba. Ahluwalia spent more time with Baba-Jee and reading holy books recommended by him than with his own family. He also changed his name to Insan (human) to shun any association with caste and religion. As Sikh militancy spread in the state, Insan stopped tucking his beard in the military style he had learned from his Army retired uncle. In white *Kurta-Pajama* (Punjabi style shirt and trousers) and white turban with a flowing beard, Insan looked like any other holy man, albeit only in appearance. In order to avoid the wrath of Sikh militants, he started offering them safe places to hide in and around the Dera. He also used his police and para-military connections to secure the release of known militants. These connections paid rich dividends when Satya Baba passed away. As the outpouring of grief continued among *Baba*'s followers, Insan finalized the plan of succession. The militants eliminated two of his main rivals to become the *Dera* chief, which paved the way for Insan's succession. Soon thereafter, he requested heavy police protection from the state to keep Sikh militants away.

Insan Baba became the chief, and under his command, the *Dera* expanded like the suburbs of North America. *Baba*'s new clout ensured that his daughter got married to a powerful politician's son. His son, Sarbjit Ahluwalia, got admission in an exclusive residential school in a hill station. The rites and rituals that were missing during Satya Baba's time came in full force. Legendary stories started appearing about Satya Baba. Insan also claimed that *Baba-Jee* had told him the exact date and time of his death; thus ensuring timely and proper succession to his mission. The followers started coming in large numbers to *Dera* on every *Punya* (the night of full moon) when Insan would enter the room of Satya Baba for an hour. The followers would stand outside chanting '*Om*'. Insan's claim was that Satya Baba had told him to meet on the night of every *Punya* to seek guidance and spiritual blessing from his soul. Every month he told a brand new story to *Sangat* about Satya Baba's blessings and advice. This is how he initiated and completed various projects on the *Dera* complex by inspiring followers to fulfill the wishes of Satya Baba. Although he appeared very healthy, Insan Baba had developed a tumor in his brain. Discovery of the deadly disease was made at the advanced stage of cancer, and Insan had only a few days to live. The family rushed to call his only son back home to deal with unforeseen succession.

Sarbjit Ahluwalia was now an engineer working with a multi-national company as a computer engineer. He rushed back, but Insan Baba had already expired. As the last rites of *Baba* were being performed, the local power blocks started playing their cards. Insan had supported Akali legislator Jagir Singh in the 2007 election, and the Congress candidate Amar Singh had avowed to take revenge. As the ceremony of succession was to start, some trustees started backing a long time *Sevadar* (volunteer) of the *Dera*-Shamsher Singh. Backed by the Congress leader Amar Singh, these opponents of Sarbjit Singh demanded an open meeting of followers to present the 'religious' credentials of both candidates. In the domain of religious and spiritual training, Sarbjit Ahluwalia was in a very shallow end of the knowledge pool. At this crucial moment, however, Jagir Singh came to his rescue with his trusted team of police and figures from the criminal underworld. A scheme was hatched by the DSP (Deputy Superintendent of Police), Rajinder Singh Thind.

A one-time field hockey player, DSP Thind was married to the daughter of a very senior police officer of ADG (Additional Director General) rank. Thus, he felt secure from the challenges of police chain of command. In addition, he had the backing of the Akali stalwart Jagir Singh. DSP Thind was always able to think outside the box. Upon his arrival, he met with his Station House Officers (SHOs) to eliminate the old percentage system worked out between the police and drug smugglers. Since the police could acquire any amount of a variety of drugs on their own, he thought it would be more profitable to sell it directly to consumers. All SHOs got marching orders to use local chemist shops with hired foot soldiers to sell drugs in the area and share the profits. A new district police chief, however, became a thorn in the backbone of the entire underworld in the district. Known for his honesty and commitment to his work, the Chief reigned heavily on all corrupt police officials and their criminal partners, including the ones from the political domain. As Jagir Singh and other elected officials felt the heat of the police Chief's honest operations, he was transferred to a peace time establishment. Although police and civil officers enjoy job security in India, the power of transfer belongs to the state executives[13]. After the Chief's departure from the district, the return to normalcy was celebrated with fanfare.

DSP Thind's plan worked perfectly to install Sarbjit as the new *Dera* chief. His chief rival, Shamsher Singh, was killed by a hitherto unknown 'Sikh terrorist' group. The law enforcement agency worked at the speed of light as it eliminated four 'terrorists' from this group in the police encounter. DSP Thind's name was recommended for a police medal for his bravery and commitment to duty. In this 'spiritual' politics of *Dera* succession, Jagir Singh's group came out victorious. Although Baba Sarbjit Singh did not give an open call in the 2012 elections to support the Akali candidate, the message was delivered to the followers in a strong, yet diplomatic manner. Garg knew about the *Dera*'s sympathy with the Akali candidate, but he was hopeful that a picture of him touching the feet of Baba-Jee in local newspapers would be worth a thousand votes. He had no idea that the 'cobra will bite you, whether you call it cobra or Mr. Cobra'[14]. *Baba-Jee* had already decided in favour of Jagir Singh in Dholpur constituency, no amount of obeisance from Garg was going to change his mind. Just before the arrival of the PPP candidate, *Baba-Jee* disappeared from the *Dera* 'for some unknown reasons.' Garg was disappointed but wanted to capitalize from this visit by, at least, meeting important members of the *Dera* management. As he sat down for a cup of tea in the VIP lounge, Garg was told that two main trustees were in a meeting with Madam Pinky.

Madam Pinky was a local socialite and head of three orphanages in the state, including one on the outskirts of Dholpur. These orphanages were run by a national charitable organisation called *Mata* (mother). Madam Pinky had no experience running charities but circumstances in her personal life had led her to hitherto unknown paths. The daughter of an Air-Force *Jawan* (soldier), Pinky was born in a military hospital. She did not stay in military station for long as her maternal uncles brought her to a major city of Punjab. They had a small but very profitable furniture manufacturing business because they were the pioneers in the area. The family enjoyed a comfortable upper middle class living and sent their children, including Pinky, to an English medium school run by a Christian charitable trust. A charming personality, Pinky became a 'beauty queen' from her early days at the school. She participated in all dance and fashion shows of her school and represented the school in state and national functions. By grade ten, Pinky was already a fully developed woman.

Pinky's first professional call came from a British Punjabi pop singer-Kuku-who was looking for dancers to make a video for his second album of songs with sexually explicit lyrics. The producer knew that Kuku neither had a voice nor any vocal training. The songs provided by an amateur writer had no poetic substance. However, the loud music by the singer's British companions, includingthe drums of Jamaican immigrants in Britain, was the backbone of his album. For a video, they needed half-naked good looking Punjabi girls to make it a success. Kuku needed a success story because he had failed in almost everything. His first album of loud music and meaningless lyrics was a flop. In a family of seven siblings, Kuku grew up in the relative comforts of a working class family in the midlands. His father worked in a steel plant and his mother in a sewing factory when she was not on maternity leave. After delivering six female babies, she gave birth to Kuku. A baby boy's birth was celebrated like the second coming of Christ. As the only boy in the family, he was raised like a prince in a working class sub-division. Kuku's father was a simple villager turned industrial worker with a keen sense of buying urban properties. He did not let his daughters study beyond school and they were married off with large dowries as teenagers. A simple industrial worker would have gone bankrupt with six dowries, but he survived with the appreciated value of numerous properties.

While the girls were not allowed to study beyond school, Kuku did not want to study in school. He wanted to become a celebrity. He had seen many successful Punjabi boys in the field of music without any talent and education. So he became a singer. Although his first album failed in the market, luck was on his side. Kuku's father died two weeks after his retirement, and now all the properties were in his mother's name. She had never refused money to young Kuku. A visiting producer from India convinced him to sell a couple of properties and invest in his second album and video. He convinced his mother and landed in India with the shining Pound Sterling's mighty exchange rate. The hired crew in India praised Kuku's singing style to the skies as he showered money

on this project. Dancing girls for the video received high payments
and Pinky was paid the highest for her beauty and dancing skills. Her
family objected but she had become an independent woman. As Punjabi
television's cultural shows flashed the femininity of her body on screens,
she started getting offers from known directors and producers in Punjab.
At the age of eighteen, she became Miss Teen Punjab. These beauty
contests became more frequent with the arrival of the cosmetic industry
in the 'liberalized' Indian market. Pinky was offered sponsorships from
the cosmetic industry to pursue a career in the entertainment industry. She
travelled abroad with 'cultural' troupes of Punjabi singers and dancers.

As the *nouveau* rich Punjabi singers established themselves in the
market, they turned their attention to the Punjabi film industry. Pinky had
her first opportunity to be an actor in Kuku's first movie, which had a
typical story of promiscuous life in the West in comparison to the cultured
life of ethics and morality in Punjab. The deep pockets of Kuku made it
possible to hire a well-known talented director and professional crew not
only in Punjab but also in England. "I don't know how to act and I have
never taken any acting lessons," Pinky told the director. She just wanted
to be modest. "Don't worry," he said, "if you knew how to act, we would
never take you in a Punjabi movie". She had never expected this sharp
reply. However, after acting in a number of Punjabi movies, she realized
that the director was not joking. As new 'talent'- younger and more
attractive bodies-started flooding the Punjabi entertainment industry,
Pinky decided to leave for a bigger market in Mumbai. By now, she
had developed a social network from Punjab to Bollywood. A socialite
friend from Delhi introduced her to a few 'insiders' in Bollywood. After
spending two years in the business and sleeping with more than a dozen
'insiders', Pinky was able to get some minor roles as an extra. She
realized that entry in Bollywood without talent was impossible unless
you were a son or a daughter of an actor, director, producer, or even a
dialogue writer. Since there was no real income and her savings did not
even last six months in the most expensive city in India, Pinky's survival
depended on her ability to sell her body.

Feeling betrayed and abused, Pinky came to Delhi to live with her
socialite friend. She introduced Pinky to a big businessman who was
ready to divorce his wife. With a new condo and a luxury car with a
driver, Pinky once again felt she had now become a part of society's
elite club. She attended and hosted kitty parties for modern urban ladies.
Every party had a theme, from childhood life to a fashion show. Just like
any human beings, these ladies also had souls. For spiritual satisfaction,

therefore, they all participated in some charity work. During social events, they praised each other for their volunteer work for the poor and for vulnerable members of society. Pinky also joined a couple of charities- an orphanage and save the tiger group. The orphanage *Mata* (mother) ran several dozen centers in various Indian cities for orphaned children. Pinky used her 'acting' and other entertainment skills to raise money for this charity. She would also join TV telethons to spread awareness about the dangers faced by tigers in India. Anytime a tiger was killed, the group would demonstrate and demand an inquiry and punishment for the guilty. Every year, tigers kill several dozen people in India. No one ever demonstrated because the victims were the poor and the tribal people of India.

Although Pinky did not own any real wealth, the life-style she was living made her part of India's urban elite. This status collapsed one early morning as she came to know that her wealthy boyfriend had no intention of divorcing his wife and that she was one of several women waiting in line for the story of his divorce to unfold. The socialite friend also felt betrayed because she had no idea about the other ladies in the businessman's life. One door had closed, but a new window of opportunity opened for Pinky. The director of *Mata*'s Punjab based three orphan centers had resigned to go and settle in Canada. Pinky was the favourite of many directors, and, as a result, she got the job. After a long absence from Punjab, she came back to her native land. This time, however, in a totally different role. Her role was not only to manage three big orphanage centers but also to raise funds for the charity. Life in Mumbai and Delhi had taught her few business skills. She registered a fund-raising company in some fictitious names. This company would sign fund raising contracts with charities and keep anything from fifty to seventy-five per cent of the collected funds. In due time, she was able to hire and fire staff in all three Mata centers.

She became a virtual dictator of the *Mata* centers. Under her command, the orphanage started taking more girls. Having spent time in charities, she was able to use clichés to convince staff members who disagreed with her new direction. "Girls are more vulnerable in society than boys," she told her staff, "since we have limited spaces, our priority must be to provide shelter to girls." Friendly staff members were also told to reject non-attractive girls and boys. In order to develop a team of trusted and reliable friends, she kept firing staff members who were opposed to the changes and 'reforms' in orphanage centers. As the team started singing from the same page, the staff at the *Mata* centers became a close knit family. Using her previous skills from the entertainment industry, Pinky developed close relations with the social, economic, and political elite in the area. Her vision was fully realized when the *Mata* orphanages became centers for prostitution. Initially, only older girls were supplied to wealthy and powerful clients for money and favours; however, as demand outpaced supply, the younger girls were also forced into the trade. Orphans were not allowed to go out even to attend school as Pinky managed to hire teachers to open on-site schools. Her connections with officers from the education department meant she had no problem with getting official recognition for such schools. Boys and girls were forced to sleep together after forcibly giving them alcohol and drugs. They were routinely beaten and mentally tortured to ensure no one ever spoke about their ordeal to each other and to outsiders.

Pinky and her team members used this ill-gotten wealth to buy properties and invest in other ventures. Madam Pinky became a 'respected' member of the social elite. She had collected more 'honours' and 'volunteer service awards' than anyone else in the area except *Baba-Jee*. And now she needed *Baba-Jee*'s help in the middle of the election campaign. The election commissioner had transferred most local civil and police officers to far-away locations. Thus, she felt her team no longer had official backing as new officers were unknown. An old social activist had been gathering information about the activities of the orphanages in association with a Chandigarh based journalist. Pinky was afraid they would use the uncertain election times to either write stories in newspapers or launch some public interest litigation (PIL) in the high court to ask for judicial inquiry into the activities of *Mata* centers. Obviously, she did not believe in the old wisdom that 'if you don't want anyone to know, don't do it'[15]. In her mind, only *Baba-Jee* with high connections could stop the activities of this dangerous duo. Thus, she decided to meet *Baba*'s lieutenants. She had, of course, previously tried to offer services of her girls to *Dera* trustees but most of them refused as their plates were full. The nursing college in the *Dera* had enough supply of young females for all of them. The manager, however, had different tastes, so he fell for Pinky's offers. It was payback time, so he assured Madam Pinky that he would convince Baba-Ji to help her.

The PPP candidate was not too happy that *Baba-Ji* disappeared from the *Dera* even though he had informed his secretary about his arrival time. Adding salt to his wounds, the *Dera* manager gave priority to Madam Pinky over a well-known financier of the area. Controlling his emotions, Garg decided to make the best of it by asking trustees to accompany him to Satya Baba's room. In all religious places in India, the VIPs always have a separate and faster entry than devotees. This *Dera* was no exception. At any given time, it could take an hour to four hours to visit Satya Baba's worship room, but VIPs entered from the exit point in seconds. Garg, accompanied by his entourage, entered the room as the devotee entry was temporarily stopped. He bowed and put his head at the feet of the small marble statue of Satya Baba. A cameraman was asked to take photos from all angels for a news release. A picture of 'humble' Garg at the feet of this revered saint would speak directly to the hearts of Baba's admirers in the constituency. His media advisor also asked him to take few more pictures doing *Seva* (volunteer work). Garg was photographed serving food to devotees and washing dishes in the *Langar* hall. Armed with these pictures, Garg sent his media person to ensure these photographs and the story of his visit would make headlines, or at least, appear on the front pages of all newspapers' local editions. He also authorized a large sum to purchase proper space for this story. As he left the Dera, Garg started dreaming about next day's headlines.

References

1. Sumanta Banerjee (1984). "Punjab: The Best Lack all Convictions, While the worst are full of Passionate Intensity." *Economic and Political Weekly*, 19 (27): 1020.
2. http://Articles.*TimesofIndia.IndiaTimes.com/2011-11-24/Chandigarh/ 30436732. Retrieved 25 August 2012.*
3. *Tehelka Magazine,16 (6), February 14, 2009.*
4. *Ibid.*
5. *Ibid.*
6. http://Articles.TimesofIndia.IndiaTimes.com/2011-11-24, op.cit.
7. Gurpreet Bal and Parmjit Judge (2010). "Innovations, Entrepreneurship and Development: A Study of the Scheduled Castes in Punjab." *Journal of Entrepreneurship*, 19(1): 43.
8. http://Articles.TimesofIndia.IndiaTimes.com/2011-11-24. op. cit.
9. *Ibid.*
10. *Ibid.*
11. An Indian proverb
12. To learn more, see W.H. McLeod (2001). *Exploring Sikhism: Aspects of Sikh Identity, Culture and Thought.* New Delhi: Oxford University Press.
13. This power has been abused by state executives to such an extent that

very few officers dare challenge the politicians. An Indian Administrative Service (IAS) officer of Haryana cadre was transferred for simply using his authority to cancel Congress President Sonia Gandhi's son-in-law's shady land deal with DLF. Known for his honesty, IAS Khemka has been transferred forty-three times in his twenty years of service. See *Times of India*, October 16, 2012.

14.   An Indian proverb.
15.   A Chinese proverb.

5

Media: The Fourth Pillar
of Corruption

*The man who reads nothing at all is better educated than the man
who reads nothing, but newspapers*
— Thomas Jefferson

The headlines were not what Garg had expected, but they created headaches for Congress candidate Amar Singh. "Five dead after drinking spurious liquor, supplied by Amar Singh Campaign," stated the headlines of two major Punjabi dailies. Amar Singh's picture under five dead bodies created panic in the Congress camp not only in Dholpur, but also in the state campaign. Although the headlines were only in the district edition of both papers, they attracted the attention of the entire state. A television channel owned by the opposition started showing the headlines on hourly breaking news. Amar Singh summoned his media and communication advisor, known simply as the Professor, to his place in the morning hours. As he started getting phone calls from state capital in the wee hours, Amar Singh exploded at the Professor: "What is your job, how are we receiving such negative headlines, and why are our stories not appearing on par with the Akali campaign?" He bombarded the Professor with questions. The Professor was still trying to recover from last night's scotch. He asked for a lime and warm water. "Sir, we did not buy the package," he replied in a low voice. He was referring to the corrupt practices of the media, in general, and the newspapers, in particular.

In a perfect world, the media is often portrayed as the fourth pillar of a liberal democratic state. As libertarian and enlightenment writers raised the banner of revolt against medieval authorities, they also demanded a clear separation of powers with checks and balances. Thus, a classical model was created in the United States by clearly defining the powers and limiting the authority of the three branches of the government; those of law making (the Congress), law implementation (the President and his cabinet), and law adjudication (the Judiciary). The rise of the media was often equated with public scrutiny of all three branches of the government. While legislated statutes and the media industry's self-regulations have enhanced the quality of scrutiny on public officials, the privatization and monopoly control of the media have also created certain challenges for the industry. Above all, the profit motive has made the media subservient to advertisement dollars; thus 'he who pays the piper calls the tune'[1]. The media has played a vital role in stilling values, beliefs, and attitudes toward politics in both constructive and destructive ways. In this context, the media in Punjab has not been any different from media in other jurisdictions.

For election purposes, the main media outlets have been vernacular newspapers and television networks. Despite India's giant status in (IT) industries, the use of this medium has still been confined to campaign 'war rooms' and metro cities. The campaign for the man on the street was carried on through conventional techniques. Despite the presence of numerous newspapers in the Punjabi language, the market has been dominated by two Jalandhar based media giants: the *Ajit* group and the *Hind Smachar* group. The story of these two media houses has also been closely related to the story of communal identities and communal politics in Punjab. Despite being one of the oldest languages in the world, the Punjabi script never developed in uniform. During the *Mughal period*, Farsi was the official language of the state even during the Sikh empire of Maharaja Ranjit Singh. The British introduced both Urdu and English through the modern school system after establishing their Raj in the nineteenth century. All three religious communities continued to speak Punjabi but used different scripts to write the language: Sikhs used *Gurmukhi*, Hindus used *Devenagri*, and Muslims used the *Shahmukhi* script. In post-independence India, Sikh leaders started associating their struggle for the Sikh-dominated Punjabi state with the *Gurmukhi* script. The use of Urdu during the British period meant, however, the number of *Gurmukhi* readers was rather small. As a result, the *Gurmukhi* newspapers had a very limited readership. In 1966, after the bifurcation of Punjab on a linguistic basis, the leading Punjabi-*Gurmukhi* paper was publishing only 8,000 copies daily, while the total circulation of *Gurmukhi* papers was 39,000[2]. In post-1966 Punjab, Punjabi in *Gurmukhi* script became the language of instruction. Needless to say, the number of Punjabi-*Gurmukhi* readers increased substantially.

In politics, the Sikh issues were presented by Punjabi-*Gurmukhi* newspapers, and the Hindu community's voice was raised by the Hindi-Urdu press. The *Hind Smachar* group was controlled by Lala Jagat Narain, a refugee from Lahore who had settled in Jalandhar and started publishing an Urdu daily. As the Punjabi Suba movement developed, the *Gurmukhi* press sided with the Sikhs and the Hindi-Urdu press defended the Indian government's position that a state on the sensitive Indo-Pak border should not be portioned on linguistic or religious grounds. In the new atmosphere of Sikh militancy from 1978 to 1993, the dividing line between the two media houses consolidated even further. As the readership increased, the Chandigarh based Tribune Trust and the Jalandhar based *Hind Smachar* groups also started publishing Punjabi-Gurmukhi dailies-*Punjabi Tribune* and *Jag Bani* respectively. The *Ajit* group openly sided with Sikh secessionists and its readership increased from 40,000 in 1978 to 100,000 in 1984[3]. The *Hind Smachar* group's *Jag Bani* grew from 20,000 to 50,000 in the same period as it defended the Indian state against Bhinderawale and his militant brigades. The Chandigarh based *Punjabi Tribune* denounced the Jalandhar based press "for partisan prejudices and trading half-truths and blatant lies" to spread communal poison[4]. Its voice of reason helped the *Punjabi Tribune* to secure a second position in the Punjabi-Gurmukhi press with 60,000 dailies in 1984. The *Jag Bani*, however, was now targeted by Sikh terrorists, as they first killed its owner Lala Jagat Narain in 1981, and then started targeting magazine stalls, transport vehicles, and hawkers associated with the *Hind Smachar* group. As a result of militant rule in Punjab, by the end of the 1980's, the *Jag Bani*'s daily circulation decreased to only 30,000[5].

In the past two decades since the return of normalcy in 1993, the media scene has changed dramatically with the rise of the private Television (TV) industry along with various national newspaper chains starting daily publications for Punjab's market. India's leading paper *Dainik Jagran* has started publishing both Hindi and Punjabi dailies in Punjab. Another noticeable change has been associated with the collapse of the government school education system and the rise of the private school industry in the state. As the private schools only teach Hindi and English, the readership of Punjabi-*Gurmukhi* has declined. As a result, even the most anti-Hindi newspapers, like the Jalandhar based *Ajit*, have started publishing daily Hindi editions. In the meantime, the television market has grown in the number of Punjabi channels and the cable network in the state. In this electronic medium, the Akali Dal has outsmarted the Congress with vast ownership not only of TV channels but also of cable networks. The Akali Dal has used its virtual monopoly over cable networks for partisan objectives. A study noted that any news channels critical of the Akali government were not allowed access to cable networks in Punjab, as the party had a virtual monopoly in the market."[6] In fact, during the election, the Punjabi Television Channel (PTC) was the only channel that had full time access to cable networks. The Congress claimed that PTC was controlled by the Badal family. The Akali Dal president, Sukhbir Singh Badal, did not deny this ownership claim but stated that it was all legal[7].

During campaigns, the media has an important role in shaping public minds, especially how politician were perceived by the people. The opposition tactics to link liquor distribution and utter disregard for human life with Amar Singh's campaign was part of its strategy to define Amar Singh in negative terms. The Akali candidate Jagir Singh believed in an offensive campaign, and as much negativity as possible. He believed in throwing enough mud on the opponent in the hope that some will stick. In general, these negative tactics worked because "they make voters mad at your opponent."[8] Of course, one has to be very careful not to be directly linked with this kind of gutter politics. If people were to find out that such stories were planted by one candidate's campaign, the mud throwing could back fire. The Akali candidate had kept his campaign at arms-length from these allegations. The story was 'picked-up' by two major newspapers after three individuals gave sworn affidavits to the reporters. They were present in the drinking party and had 'known' that the liquor was supplied by Amar Singh's supporters. Jagir Singh was quoted in a different story asserting the moral high ground with a suggestion that all liquor should be banned during campaigns and that distilleries should be shut down.

For Amar Singh, this story was a temporary diversion from the campaign trail. He had learned from his sources that liquor related deaths had nothing to do with any campaign. Since there were so many unauthorized illicit liquor distilleries in the village and towns using all kinds of chemicals to speed up the fermentation process, liquor related deaths had become a routine story. A few days before the election-day, however, this sinister story was not normal for Amar Singh. He dispatched his treasurer Mohan and the Professor to deal with media representatives. After hearing a mouthful from Amar Singh, the Professor justified his inability to deal with the media's insatiable thirst for more money. He had spoken with media representatives months in advance and gave the figures to Amar Singh. The Congress candidate, however, was too busy in dealing with his own party. Since party nominations were to be decided by the national leadership in Delhi, all prospective Congress candidates were in the nation's capital while their opponents were campaigning. By the time the national leadership decided to nominate Congress candidates, they had barely three weeks to campaign in their respective constituencies. This uncertainty meant most Congress candidates started their campaigns weeks, if not months, after their main opponents.

There was, however, no time for 'I told you so'. Mohan and the Professor started their task of dealing with media representatives. The priority was to deal with both major newspapers published in Punjabi and Hindi. The Professor, of course, had heard the rates long before the campaign but never finished the deal because Amar Singh failed to make a decision. The Congress campaign was paying the reporters and the regional bureau chiefs on a daily basis for every story. Since the opponent had purchased the 'package', he had the upper hand. Both papers had asked for ₹16 *Lakh* (1.6 million) each for a full package, which included full coverage of the campaign with pictures, a few columns highlighting the achievements of the candidate, blocking any negative coverage about the campaign and the candidate, and a few small 'paid' advertisements for the purposes of generating receipts to comply with spending limits. It was ironic that the 'package' for each paper was similar to the total spending limit imposed by the Election Commission on every candidate during assembly elections. As a result, every winning MLA would begin his or her assembly membership with a lie given in a sworn affidavit to state that he or she did not exceed the spending limits. Such ethical considerations have never crossed any candidates mind either during campaign or after victory. The only issue in a campaign is to win.

The bureau chief of the major vernacular newspaper was a short and sharp man. Simply known as a Kavi (a poet), nobody in public knew his real name, Sukhpreet. Kavi had established himself in this area not only as a journalist but also as a wheeler-dealer. One could meet any civil or police official through Kavi. Known for his ability to keep all secrets, he had earned the title of a trusted middleman of government officials indulging in briberies. He met officials in complete secrecy keeping in mind that 'there were always ears on the other side of the wall'[9]. Although he had obtained his first job as a local reporter with his father's connections, Kavi had proven himself as an able manager in news business. His father was a school teacher and a known poet who wrote poetry for the Punjabi newspaper's special Sunday editions. He was also well known for his sycophancy in literary circles. He would often write poems praising people in powerful positions. Critics called it a low point when he even wrote poems praising the dog of a newspaper owner. Thus, Kavi's relationship with the owners of the newspaper was based on two generations of family loyalty.

"During elections, all news and opinions are tightly controlled by the owners and chief editor," said Kavi, as Mohan and the Professor sat down in his office. He wanted to convey the message that the local bureau was not responsible for this negative headline. "Your opposition has not only bought a full package but continues to spend additional money for more coverage in the main edition which covers the entire state." Apparently the package only guaranteed news in the local district edition in which all nine constituencies of the parliamentary seat were covered. "Although there are only few days left in the campaign," said Kavi, "these are crucial times. In addition to the cost of full package, you need another 4 to 5 *Lakh* for special coverage. Some of that money would go toward 'damage control' from today's negative news." He sounded like an impressive used car salesman. Kavi had learned through experience that a business approach was primary, and news stories were secondary in media business. In a country of 1.2 billion people, there was no shortage of news at any given time; the point, however, was to run a profitable business. The Congress team knew very well that they had no choice but to buy the 16 *Lakh* package to avoid future damage to the campaign, but they were still not convinced about the additional costs.

"Our paper is very popular in the countryside," said Kavi. "The Akali Dal has its stronghold in villages, so it's here that you need to convince the voters to vote for an alternative. Further, most of the *Dalit* voters live in villages. If the Congress campaign is weak then they will go to the BSP." He was now speaking like an election strategist. He understood that Amar Singh's team would buy the basic package, while still being reluctant on additional costs. Kavi was going to receive only a small percentage of the package money, and most of his share was in additional money. Thus, he needed to be forceful on extra costs. He told the Congress team how he would send an 'investigation' team to the site of the liquor tragedy and report in tomorrow's main edition that Amar Singh's campaign had nothing to do with these deaths. Furthermore, the newspaper would publish Amar Singh's statement that he did not believe in the distribution of liquor during election campaigns. After a hard bargain, the Congress team reached a deal- the package plus 10,000 ₹cash on a daily basis to the local bureau. Mohan and the Professor were in a hurry to leave and meet the representatives of other papers, but Kavi insisted that they must listen to a couple of his new poems.

After listening to some worthless poetry, Mohan and the Professor moved to the office of another newspaper chain. This chain also published both Hindi and Punjabi editions but the Hindi edition was most popular in Punjab and in the neighbouring states. The bureau chief was in the office waiting for the Congress duo. In an indirect fashion, he was related to Mohan's wife. Pardeep Pandey was a trained journalist with a degree from a prestigious university. In addition to this, Pandey was now working on an on-line MBA from a bogus university in North America. The university dishes out bachelors, masters, and doctorate degrees for 'life experience'. Punjabis are obsessed with titles. A person who can manage to teach in a college for two weeks will add the title of full Professor to his name for the rest of his life. Any quack who can perform first aid will be Doctor forever. If nothing else works, a Punjabi will be known as '*Pradhan-Jee*' (honourable chief). Pandey knew he did not learn anything, but a title from a foreign university for only ₹ 25,000 was priceless. He did not feel the need to learn about the market economy from any university. In fact, no Harvard business school could compete with his real life experience as a journalist, which had taught him so much about business in India.

Relative or not, Pandey cited the same figure of ₹ 16 *Lakh* for the package to Mohan and the Professor. As he explained additional costs for the main edition and the coverage for 'damage control,' he sounded like Kavi. Mohan joked in the Professor's ears: "India needs a Competition Bureau to prevent bribe fixing." They both laughed as Pandey continued his sales pitch. "The main readership of our papers is in urban areas, and among Hindu communities in villages," said Pandey. "In the absence of the BJP, the urban community, in general, and the Hindu community, in particular, will vote for the Congress. In the past, your opponents in fact have accused us of being pro-Congress. Needless to say, it makes more sense for you to rely on our newspapers rather than others that are read by die-hard Akali voters," he continued. Pandey's shift from a business salesman to political analyst showed what qualities were required to be a journalist in India. The Congress team had no choice but to buy the package and offer Pandey no more and no less than they had offered to Kavi. Hence the same deal- the package plus ₹ 10,000 cash per diem for the local bureau. Pandey brought some sweets and congratulated the Congress team in advance for victory. "Our surveys show a clear Congress victory in the state, and Sardar Amar Singh Jee will have a major portfolio in the cabinet," said Pandey with conviction. For extra friendship and validation of his relationship with Mohan, Pandey told the Congress team that he would be able to get the Amar Singh campaign covered by *Doordarshan* (India's Public Television) in a friendly fashion. "Since I knew the regional director, the cost would be very reasonable," said the bureau chief.

As Mohan and the Professor left Pandey's office, they encountered a sub-editor of a 'feminist' magazine. Although no real feminist would ever have agreed with the pictures and content of this sexy and flashy magazine, the publisher and all-women editorial staff insisted that they represented a new wave of feminism. The sub-editor, Seema Kaur, was so beautiful and attractive that the Congress duo could not refuse her sales pitch. Since she had no office, all three decided to sit in a tea shop. The Professor had already apprised Amar Singh of two main deals over his mobile phone. He did not, however, want to mention this meeting with Seema. "You are wasting your time with old style newspapers read only by *Burehs* (a derogatory term for senior citizens)," stated this modern feminist. "The younger generation," she continued, "is looking for a fresh perspective and modern views, which our weekly presents with pictures and stories." Apart from a couple of local stories and profiles of attractive females, the magazine was basically a cut and paste from various online sites related to Bollywood and Hollywood. For its local content, the magazine had recently profiled charity hero and philanthropist, Madam Pinky. All published pictures of Pinky in the article were from her teen years.

Seema had her own analytical views. "Since our magazine is read by younger and modern people, a profile of a secular party's candidate will bring a lot of new votes for you," stated Seema. "These Akalis and BJP types are religious Taliban, *Yaar* (friend). The modern generation is against them anyway," she reasoned. The Congress duo did not hear anything because they were too busy watching Seema's body, and its language, as she burst into laughter. As they say 'when a woman laughs, an experienced man will know how much it will cost him'[10] Mohan understood very well and quickly finished his tea to leave. It was, however, a different story with the Professor. If it had been for the Professor to decide, he would have given 16 Lakh to Seema and nothing to the other two newspaper chains. He knew, however, that

Amar Singh would not agree to give a penny for this magazine. As the Professor finished his tea, the duo asked for permission to leave. "We'll be in touch with you," said the Professor unconvincingly. "I know what some people say about our magazine....Oh, it's vulgar! Its half pornography, and other bullshit," said Seema in an angry tone. "Yet, all these people and their children keep our magazine in their bedrooms...hypocrisy...eh!"

Mohan and the Professor still had a few more meetings with other reporters from minor newspapers, but a call from campaign headquarters interrupted their schedule. They had to go back to meet a reporter and a photographer from a national English daily published from Delhi. The reporter was a medium built dark man who introduced himself simply as Kumar, and his photographer as Vijay. His full name was Sidarath Kumar belonging to the state of Bihar state. The habit of only mentioning his last name perhaps came from his upbringing in a military environment. Kumar's father was an army officer in the Military Engineering Services (MES- otherwise known as money earning services) branch. His colleagues had expected him to rise to the top echelons of the military chain-of-command, but he was forced to step down as a full Colonel after an internal inquiry found that he was involved in a massive scandal of fraudulent dealings and briberies related to construction material. Kumar neither pursued a career in the military nor fulfilled the dream of his father to become an IAS officer. Just as his father settled in Delhi to start a new career as a businessman in the construction industry, Kumar joined Delhi University. He obtained graduate degrees in English literature and journalism from Delhi. Unlike most of his classmates, Kumar was familiar with various regions of India largely because of his father's different postings. As a result, he had no problem in covering stories in all parts of India for the leading English daily that hired him immediately after graduation. He was also very familiar with Punjab and Punjabis because most of the officers in the Indian army hailed from this region and the Delhi region has a large Punjabi population.

Kumar was on his new assignment in Punjab to cover assembly elections, and he demanded to see Amar Singh for an interview. However, he wanted to brief the campaign communication team about the importance of this assignment. He knew that every candidate in Punjab was focused on vernacular newspapers read by the masses, and that nobody had an interest in any English dailies. English newspapers were for the chattering class in India. The members of this class read the entire English newspaper from news to columns and editorials. Thus, most opinions of the chattering class are based on English newspapers and English news channels. In the Punjab assembly election, it hardly mattered what the chattering class said about campaigns. Kumar knew this, but he had to sell his own story. He decided to sit alone in a corner room with Mohan and the Professor. Kumar was well aware of the culture of sycophancy in political parties. Thus, he knew what nerve to pinch to give sensation to the entire body of the Congress duo. "Our newspaper is read on a daily basis by Mrs. Sonia Gandhi," said Kumar in a low and convincing voice. "A story about Amar Singh Jee's campaign," he continued, "will catch the eyes of the Congress supremo. I will write the story in such a way to portray Amar Singh Jee as one of the most original and innovative campaigners in modern times. If you look at the Congress leaders in Delhi, most of them are useless sycophants. I know for a fact that Mrs. Gandhi is looking for dynamic leaders. This story will go a long way in promoting Amar Singh Jee in the eyes of the Congress leadership." Mohan and the Professor's jaws dropped as they started imagining Amar Singh as a central cabinet minister.

After offering his political analysis on the career of Amar Singh, Kumar had to convince them to make an investment. "Look," as Kumar drew their attention once again toward his serious proposal, "the Akali candidates are lucky, they can directly approach the party leadership to secure nominations. The Congress candidates have several layers to cross to reach the party leadership in Delhi. It's like feudal Europe, where a trader had to pay tariffs to cross borders after a few miles. Thus, the price of a commodity travelling from Paris to Milan would go up several times. The Akalis don't have to travel that far; thus they only pay at one toll booth." Mohan understood Kumar's metaphor very well. As Amar Singh's trusted man, he had to handle the funds to secure a party nomination. "Now, just imagine," continued Kumar, "if Amar Singh Jee had a direct link with party leadership, he would not have to go through these toll booths. Not only would he be able to secure a nomination quickly, but the party leadership's blessing would mean a lucrative cabinet portfolio."

Although Kumar had not given any monetary proposal, Mohan understood his intent very well. He spoke with Amar Singh and established a threshold. After haggling in private, both Kumar and Mohan agreed on a price tag of ₹ 50,000. Mohan also told Kumar and his photographer that Amar Singh would not be able to meet them that night because his schedule was very tight. "The last rally would not end 'till 9:30 pm," said Mohan, "and after that he needs at least two to three hours to meet individuals at their homes. In Punjab, there are so many minor players with big egos. Each one requires special attention of the candidate; thus, no serious candidate is able to sleep during the campaign." Here, a politician has to be 'the first to the field and the last to the coach'[11]. "Don't worry," replied Kumar, "we've witnessed the same in almost every region of India. Big egos require big maintenance." The English daily duo agreed to meet with Amar Singh early in the morning. "We are very tired," said Kumar. "Please bring a bottle of whisky and some non-veg snacks. For dinner, we will have *Roti* (bread) with simple *Masoor Daal* (red lentil)."

Amar Singh's sleeping time never exceeded three hours during campaigns. He woke up at the rooster's first call at four in the morning. Like most Punjabis, he also recited the Lord's Prayer in the morning during these testing times. As the reporter and his photographer arrived at six in the morning, he was fully ready for his daily campaign. "In my story," Kumar began his journalistic work, "an interview with you in addition to my observations of your innovative campaign will form the central thesis. Thus, if you don't mind, I will ask some simple questions... who is likely to form the government in Punjab?" Amar Singh was very happy with this question. "All signs point to a Congress victory," said the Congress candidate. "Under Mrs. Sonia Gandhi-Jee's leadership, the Congress has led the developmental work all over India. The Akali Dal tried to take credit for the Central funds for the state's development, but now they are being exposed by the Congress. No incumbent government has ever won in Punjab so history is also on our side. Shri Rahul Gandhi-Jee has mobilized the entire youth of Punjab, and they are leading the campaign from the front. There is no doubt in my mind that Congress will form the next government to carry on developmental work under Mrs. Sonia Gandhi Jee and Shri Rahul Gandhi-Jee's leadership." As soon as Amar Singh finished his first answer, Kumar threw another question at him. "Your opponents blame the Congress for the 1984 anti-Sikh riots," asked Kumar, Amar Singh did not even allow Kumar to finish his question and asked him to turn off the tape recorder.

"My intention Amar Singh Jee is not to embarrass you and your party," Kumar was quick to add. "After all, our newspaper is well known for its editorial support for the Congress party and the Nehru-Gandhi family," he continued. Kumar had known, however, that the Congress party and its leadership did not like questions about the Sikh massacres of 1984 in Delhi and other places in the wake of Mrs. Indira Gandhi's assassination. Every commission and investigative agency report blamed the massacres on some Congress leaders who not only incited rioters but also led the mobs against innocent Sikh civilians[12]. In his defence, Kumar told Amar Singh that Congress spokesmen were well trained by foreign public relation (PR) firms to circumvent such questions. "If you listen to spokesmen of national parties," Kumar began his public relations course: "you will notice that they speak in English, so most Indians will not understand. Secondly, they will never answer any question. In fact, they are trained to give their own answers- what is often referred to as 'staying in the message box'. Thirdly, they believe that offense is the best defensive policy. For example, the question I asked can be answered by going on the offensive." Now, he got Amar Singh's full attention. "How would they answer this question," asked Amar Singh. "Just listen," replied Kumar, "The Congress party is a secular party. We don't believe in creating any divisions among people based on caste, religion, region or language. The Akali Dal and BJP are communal parties based on religious identities. As a result, they have always created tensions and riots based on religion. They practice the politics of division. The people of Punjab suffered for more than a decade and a half from such communal politics of the Akali Dal. More recently, the BJP government organised carnage against Muslims in Gujarat....My point is that those who accuse us of communalism should study their own deeds. The Congress has always been a secular party and will remain secular."

Amar Sigh was impressed with this short lesson on public relations. Kumar the entrepreneur was quick to pounce on the Congress candidate's vulnerability: "Sir, a friend of mine is a partner in a very well-known PR firm in Delhi. In fact, it's a branch of a larger multinational based in New York. Now time is short and busy for you; but after the elections, we can organize some lessons. You have great potential in politics not only in Punjab but also in the central government. Once you are trained by these PR professionals, no one will be able to match your skills. PR professionals can spin anything with their communication skills. For example, a public relations firm can convince people that coal and petrol are good for the environment. And solar and wind power would choke us to death." Amar Singh would have loved to have started these lessons now but the campaign team had already knocked on the door several times. Kumar knew Amar Singh was getting late for his campaign. As he wrapped up his recording device and the photographer took some pictures of Amar Singh, Kumar told the Congress candidate that he would finish his story by noon, well before the deadline. Amar Singh wanted to read the story before submission. "Sir, once I am done, we can call you and we'll meet with you," said Kumar. "You can read the story on my lap-top." Amar Singh asked if Kumar could email the story. "That is against journalistic ethics," replied Kumar. "Nobody would ever know you had read my story, but email would leave a permanent track." Amar Singh agreed as his entire team entered the room. Several small meetings had to be addressed before Amar Singh's grand appearance as the chief guest at a Non-Resident Indian (NRI) organized Kabbadi tournament in the late afternoon.

References

1. An English proverb.
2. Robin Jeffrey. "Indian Languages Newspapers: Punjabi-the Subliminal Change". *Economic and Political Weekly*, Volume 32 (9), March 1, 1997, p. 443.
3. *Ibid.*, p. 444.
4. *Ibid.*, p. 445.
5. *Ibid.*, p. 445.
6. Manjit Singh. "A Re-Election in Punjab and the Continuing Crisis." *Economic and Political Weekly*, Volume 47 (13), March 31, 2012, p. 21.
7. *Indian Express*, October 4, 2011.
8. David Doak (1998). "Negative Ads: Rethinking the rules." In *The Road to Victory*. Edited by Ron Faucheux, Dubuque, Iowa: Kendall/Hunt Publishing, p. 398.
9. A Chinese proverb.
10. An Indian proverb.
11. A Chinese proverb.
12. Shinder Purewal (2000). *Sikh Ethnonationalism and the Political Economy of Punjab*. New Delhi: Oxford, pp. 134-35.

6

The Non-Resident Indian Campaign

Whenever I start feeling too arrogant... I always take a trip to the U.S. The immigration guys kick the star out of my stardom

– Shahrukh Khan

Call it a coincidence, but both major candidates decided to attend NRI (Non-Resident Indians) functions that day. The Congress candidate was to be honoured at a Kabbadi[1] tournament organized by a drug smuggler NRI from the United States. And the Akali candidate, Jagir Singh, accompanied by NRI Amrik Singh, was on his way to attend a fake marriage between a Canadian NRI bride and an Indian groom for immigration purposes. Both candidates had a lot at stake in these functions because a large number of NRIs had gathered during these important final days of the campaign. As more than two million Punjabis live abroad, many campaigns for Punjab assembly and *Lok Sabha* (parliament) seats begin in London, Toronto, Vancouver and, California. While the Punjabi Diaspora is spread all over the world, three-fourth of its strength, however, is concentrated in just three countries-Canada, the United Kingdom and the United States. In Punjab politics, the contributions of the NRI segment is important in three ways; firstly, many are still Indian citizens, thus eligible to vote in Indian elections; secondly, their financial contribution is enormous despite Indian Election laws' ban on foreign contributions; and thirdly, they have family members and relatives who can be influenced to vote in a certain fashion. As a result, all political parties try to woo NRIs to support their candidates in the state.

It is not only in Punjab but in several other Indian states as well where NRIs play a major role in generating both political and financial support for the states. Overall, the Indian Diaspora is an important source of remittance to India, thus boosting its foreign reserves[2]. A study on remittances shows that some ten million overseas Indians send money to their family and extended relatives in India on a regular basis[3]. According to the World Bank, in the fiscal year of 2011-12, NRI remittance to India was 62 billion US dollars, which would likely reach 75 billion US dollars in the fiscal year of 2012-13[4]. The three largest sources of this remittance are North America, the Middle East, and Europe. In the fiscal year of 2011-12, the North American and Middle Eastern Indian Diaspora contributed 35 per cent each, and the European NRIs contribution was at 15 per cent of the total[5]. For the states of Kerala, Goa, and Punjab with a large Diaspora population, the NRI remittances are a major portion of their GDP with 30 per cent, 20 per cent and 10 per cent respectively[6]. The NRI remittance expected in the fiscal year of 2012-13 is larger than the GDP of more than two-third of the members of the United Nations. In addition, NRIs are a source of India's link with other countries in trade, politics, and diplomacy. Needless to say, the Indian government is pleased with such enormous contribution of its sons and daughters abroad. In recognition of this importance, the Indian government begins each year by organizing a *Pravasi Bhartya Divas* (Indian Diaspora Day) with a conference.

'Where the sun shines, there is also a shade'[7]. Not all children of India send happy news to the motherland. Two groups, in particular, have caused major headaches to the Indian government the Kashmiri and Sikh secessionists. The power behind these two groups has been India's traditional rival, Pakistan. Many people in Western democracies have understood Pakistan's role in supporting Kashmiri secessionists because it controlled one-third of the Kashmiri territory wrested from India in the 1947-48 war. But few have ever understood Pakistan's role in fomenting the Sikh secessionist movement against India[8]. Evidence from studies indicate that Pakistan's ISI supported the Sikh secessionist movement abroad beginning with the London based Panchi led Sikh Home Rule in the early 1960s and then Khalistani organisations from 1969 onward[9]. After losing Bangladesh (what used to be East Pakistan) in a war with India in 1971, Pakistan intensified its efforts to cause domestic trouble in India with a view to annex the rest of Kashmir. While Pakistani officials knew that Khalistan was a tall order, they continued to support terrorist activities in Punjab to create problems for Indian security forces. The problem in Punjab would mean less military force in Kashmir, the real target of Pakistani foreign policy. It would also mean that supply lines would be disrupted to the Jammu and Kashmir regions, which would clear the way for Kashmiri secessionists to launch coordinated attacks against India and would intensify the struggle to separate and join Pakistan[10]. During the cold war environment, the western liberal democracies turned a blind eye to the activities of Sikh terrorist networks. It was only after they bombed an Air India flight en route from Toronto to Delhi in June 1985 killing 329 Canadians that most western governments started taking serious note of Sikh secessionists. In the post-9/11 world, most western governments have come to understand the terrorist threats faced by India from abroad. As a result, many Sikh terrorist organisations have now been banned by London, Ottawa and Washington.

In the Dholpur constituency, Sikh NRIs have a major presence. NRI Amrik Singh, who was now sitting in the back seat of the Akali candidate Jagir Singh's SUV, was part of the Sikh secessionist movement and a member of a now banned terrorist group. Publicly known by his 'Canadian' name Mike, he was born Satwant Singh in a family of a small farmer in a relatively large village in the Dholpur electoral district. As the juggernaut of the Green Revolution rolled over the northern states of Punjab, Haryana, and eastern Uttar Pradesh (UP), small farmers found it difficult to stay in the farming sector. The new era of farm machinery, fertilizers, pesticides and insecticides had pushed the costs of agriculture higher and higher. It was not viable for small and marginal farmers to adopt such expensive inputs that were required to produce high yield varieties of crops. While the Green Revolution increased food production and incomes of large landholders, it made the small and marginal farmers simple paupers. This period corresponded with a high level of emigration from Punjab. A large number of Punjabi youth migrated to Canada, the United States, and the United Kingdom. Others ended up labouring in the booming construction of the Middle East after the formation of the OPEC (Organisation of the Petroleum Exporting Countries).

Mike's father found a new way to supplement his family income by producing and selling country made liquor. On the complaint of a local government liquor store owner, however, he was arrested along with his brother and two sons, including Mike. Mike was only seventeen at the time and in grade nine. While most of his class mates were fourteen, Mike's failure rate had made him the oldest kid in the class. It took several months and an acre of family land to drop all charges against the family. Now 18-years old, high school drop-out Mike had even fewer chances to succeed in life. Following a trend among the village youth, Mike's family decided to borrow money to send him to Dubai. A number

of village youth had already found employment in the Middle East.
Mike landed in one of Dubai's port city construction sites. A number
of Pakistani, Bangladeshi, and Indian youth were employed by western
firms to perform manual labour. In India, Mike had seen Dubai return
village boys with flashy clothes, tape recorders, and modern hair styles.
In his dreams before coming to Dubai, he had imagined a utopian vision
of clean cities with money hanging from tree branches. In reality, life was
back-breaking work filled with humiliation and indignities during the
day, and roaming rats as large as village cats at night under tents where
all labourers slept. After paying for food, shelter, and the contractor's
share, the savings were so meagre that Mike realized he would never be
able to fulfill his dream of buying back his family's land and paying off
the family debts.

An entrepreneurial mind, the necessities of life, or simply a lack
of moral and ethical values opened a new door for Mike to supplement
his income. 'The eyes do not see what the mind does not want'[11]. Mike
joined a group of illegal distillers in the area to supply liquor to labourers
on these construction sites. He had acquired these skills from his father.
In six months, he was able to send enough money to pay family debts
and buy more land than they had sold in the past. All good or bad things
come to an end. A dispute over money led to the killing of a Pakistani man
in the group. Along with seven others, Mike was arrested and charged
with murder. All of those charged were Hindus and Sikhs from India,
and the murdered man was a Muslim from Pakistan. In the desert land
where non-Muslims were forced to the end of a line even for ordering
food, justice was like a mirage. All eight were found guilty and before
the sentence could be pronounced a Sikh philanthropist stepped in to pay
blood money to the family of the Pakistani man and this settled the issue.
All charged in the murder were deported back to India. Upon returning to
his village, Mike found that Sikh militancy had engulfed the entire state.
He stopped cutting his hair and within a few months became a baptized
Khalsa Sikh.

Out of religious faith or the knocking opportunity to realize his dream
of a gangsters' lifestyle, Mike joined a militant organisation involved
in robberies, kidnappings, and murders to 'weaken' the enemies of the
Sikh community. Although most of this militant organisation's victims
were Sikhs, these warriors of Khalistan believed anyone who was not
with them was against them. Therefore, it was just to kill and terrorize
such people. A new prosperity came to Mike's family and it was noticed
by all people in the village. No one, however, dared open his mouth in

fear of retaliation. Mike's name struck terror in the hearts and minds of not only the folks from his village but from the entire surrounding area. This warrior, who could hardly qualify to become a private in the army, was now a Lieutenant-General in his group. The group had carried out several successful robberies, kidnappings, and murders. However, the news surprised many when five top 'commanders' of the group were killed in 'encounters' by para-military forces. Only a few days after these encounters, an attempt on Mike's life by his own group failed. He had become a police informer and set up his own colleagues for 'encounters'. At this crucial moment, a police officer helped Mike to get an Indian passport to flee India. His original passport was in his real name, Satwant Singh. A new fake identity in the name of Amrik Singh was created to obtain a brand new passport. After landing in Canada, Amrik Singh became Mike.

Just like most other illegal immigrants, Mike filed a refugee application. A great international convention to provide protection to people fleeing from religious, ethnic, political and other types of persecution has been widely misused in Canada. A sense of guilt from the World War II period has prevented Canada from tightening the loop holes in the system. The Jewish refugees fleeing Hitler's genocide were refused entry by the Liberal Prime Minister of Canada, Mackenzie King. Now even criminals fleeing justice can apply for refugee status. Mike had not only applied for refugee status in Canada, but crossed over to the United States and filed an application under asylum laws. Still not satisfied, he also managed a fake marriage with a Canadian citizen for 20,000 dollars. The rates of such transactions were relatively cheaper in the 1980s compared with today, and the process to obtain legal status was also much faster. As he became a permanent resident, Mike withdrew his refugee applications both in Canada and the United States. Now, he was free to join his 'militant' brethren to enrich himself.

Lesson number one for Mike was the realization that hard work without education meant an average lifestyle in Canada. He had dreams beyond an average worker's imagination. Although his association with militant groups meant access to temple funds and free trips to Pakistan, he was not satisfied with his income levels. On the positive side, however, he had developed close relations with people who shared his vision of grandeur in life. Along with two other militant friends, Mike was perhaps a pioneer in opening construction companies even during recessionary times with the help of drug money. For a drug dealer's gang, the main problem was to turn cash into legal white money. Mike provided a solution by investing all that cash in construction companies and sharing the profits in legal money. He also opened various small businesses, including a pizza chain, for money laundering. Drug money came to fill the coffers of these cash-based businesses, and this enormous income helped boost the re-sale value of these businesses. Mike was once sued by someone who bought his pizza chain with inflated incomes. After purchasing, the new owner realized the real income was not even one-tenth of what Mike's company had been filing with Revenue Canada. The case was dropped after the drug dealer's muscle men visited the new owner at his house after midnight.

Mike and his friends' biggest and safest investments were in the field of Canadian politics. From municipal to provincial and federal levels, the group worked together as a team with almost every major political party in Canada. They used their temples and organisations to make members for political nominations, and party leadership races. Investing their own money, they delivered political power to numerous politicians on a platter. Once in office, these politicians delivered favours to their supporters. At municipal levels, the construction companies received favours in developing on any property. If any by-laws hindered the process, the politicians were quick to adapt. From provincial governments, the money for 'community projects', opening new bogus colleges to bring international students, getting appointments to important boards and commissions, and opening gambling casinos. In one province, the group has benefited enormously from its 'agricultural land' reservation policy. While ordinary farmers have difficulty getting permission to build even a second house for their children on their farms, Mike and his team have converted several hundred acres of agricultural land to industrial, commercial, and residential property. At the federal levels, the group has had close connections with every immigration minister of every ruling party. They have become masters of human smuggling operations in Canada.

As the Akali candidate Jagir Singh and Mike arrived at the marriage palace, a large group of NRI's and immigration consultants came out to greet the duo. The marriage palace was famous for organizing fake marriages for the purposes of emigration. As immigration authorities in various western countries tightened their rules to ensure only bona fide spouses were sponsored, the human smuggling operatives found ways to circumvent those rules. Immigration officials insist on seeing actual photographs and DVD's of the wedding with religious ceremonies and wedding parties. The owners of this marriage palace arrange everything, from a religious ceremony in a nearby temple to a full reception with orchestra and invited guests. The NRI woman getting married today was a prime example of the type of clientele the palace caters to. She had been sponsored by a Canadian 'groom' on an exchange basis. After settling and divorcing him, she had to sponsor the groom's cousin as her new husband. The process took several years, but she was able to obtain Canadian citizenship and sponsor her parents and four siblings during those years including meeting her 'exchange' obligations. Although she finally wanted to marry for real and settle down, she and her four siblings found 'fake marriage' offers they could not reject. For five marriages, the family had made a cool half million dollars. Hard working Canadian families will never see that amount in cash in their lives. The corrupt and flawed immigration laws of Canada have made these types of immigrants instant millionaires.

The human smugglers gathered at this 'marriage' were masters of their domain. Several ran vocational schools and companies that existed on paper only to provide credentials and work experience to prospective immigrants. One may not know how to change the light bulb, but these consultants could provide you with a diploma, or even a degree, with several years of experience as an electrician or an electrical engineer. Others could create documents to show that a homeless person in fact was a multi-millionaire with properties all over the state to obtain a visitor's visa. They could obtain clearance certificates from police to provide a clean chit to persons charged with serious crimes. As medical clearance has been one of the requirements from various immigration authorities, these consultants work with embassy designated physicians to clear cases with serious illness, including cancer. There have never been any moral and ethical guidelines in this human smuggling industry, but profits are enormous. A portion of this profit has always been invested in politics in both India and abroad, especially in Canada. Jagir Singh has known this industry very well because he had approached these consultants in the past to manage visas for the children of his supporters. In addition, Mike had collected money from these consultants for the Akali candidate in every campaign. For this campaign, Mike had managed ₹ 1 Crore (ten million) from his contacts in Canada and India. Jagir Singh thanked all the 'honourable' guests who had gathered at the marriage palace and gave his blessings to the 'newlyweds' before departing on his regular campaign tour.

Congress candidate Amar Singh was asked to reach the tournament grounds at three in the afternoon, but the campaign commitments kept him away until six in the evening. It was dark but thanks to the NRI Jagga's deep pockets, the Kabbadi grounds were illuminated by powerful flood lights. The organizers had conveyed to Amar Singh that the final match would end by 3:30 pm and the prize distribution would start immediately after the match. Thanks to Indian Standard Time, however, the final match had not started even at 6pm. Jagga and company gave a fitting welcome to Amar Singh with slogans and a live band. The Kabbadi tournament was an annual affair organized by Jagga's youth club in the village. In his youth, Jagga was a known Kabbadi player in Punjab. His father ran a dairy farm in the village. As a result, Jagga's upbringing did not lack nutrition. He did not do well in school but in the field of Kabbadi Jagga was an Einstein. He was not only physically powerful but also very smart with playing tactics. It was this field that opened the doors to future fortunes and misfortunes.

Jagga was selected in a Kabbadi team to play in an international tournament in California organized by a Punjabi gangster and drug lord. Since passengers on trans-Atlantic flights were allowed two large suitcases, Jagga was asked to pack his clothes in one suitcase, and carry the second belonging to the organizers. He was told that the organizing committee chief's wife runs a *Sari* and Punjabi clothing shop in California, so the second suitcase was for her. It was only upon landing in San Francisco that Jagga realized that the second suitcase was full of *Saris* and heroin. Despite his innocent pleas and his naming of the tournament chief in his statements, Jagga was sentenced to five years in jail. While in jail, he received death threats from the Kabbadi chief for naming him during the trial. Jagga knew that he would be deported upon his release and killed by the drug dealer in India. Thus, he spent 5 years building connections with drug dealers and gangsters in jail. The connections proved valuable as he was deported back to India. He got a new passport under a false name, made a deal with a powerful Punjabi drug dealer to supply opium and heroin to his American connections, and landed in Mexico. From Mexico, he was taken to Montreal, Canada on a visitor's visa. Gang connections arranged a 'marriage of convenience' and got him Canadian Permanent residency within months while Jagga worked to create Punjabi connections for his Mexican associates. From Montreal, he moved to Brampton, Ontario for business purposes. His next stop took him to Vancouver, British Columbia, an important hub for drug smuggling in North America. After successfully recruiting truck companies and truck drivers for drug transportation, he moved to California. He was asked to keep a low profile, and he was very successful at maintaining invisibility.

He was a great asset to his gang. In addition to the charge of bringing opium and heroin from Punjab to Central America, he was quick to establish connections with the Punjabi American trucking community to transport drugs within the US and across North American borders. This transport network was engaged in importing high potency Canadian marijuana into the US market, and exporting South American cocaine to Canada. For centuries, immigrants from all over the world have arrived on the shores of the United States to build one of the most powerful economies of the world. In the process of building this great country, many generations of these immigrants have realized their American dreams of living in freedom, liberty, and prosperity. Jagga, or Brown Jack as he was known in his gang, was pursuing his American dream by destroying the lives of North American youth. Jagga became rich beyond imagination but his illegal status in the US was a Damocles sword on his head. As a result, he had moved most of his assets to India and Canada. Although he got married to a Sikh American citizen from his new neighbourhood, he could not apply for a green card. Despite his residency in the US, however, he was able to obtain his Canadian citizenship with the help of a consultant.

Business was flourishing for Jagga, but the clouds of danger were always on the horizon. Gang members were at risk of either an arrest or death all the time. It was a routine part of the business. Suddenly, a number of Jagga's Punjabi associates came under attack from a rival Canadian gang. Three truck drivers were killed within a week. While Jagga kept the façade of a gangster, he was, in fact, a coward. He was fearful of his own life and had sleepless nights. He knew that it was easy to enter a gang but difficult to leave. His wife convinced him to leave everything and move back to India. He moved all assets to his native village and a nearby city in Punjab. In India, this ill-gotten wealth earned him a new title- a philanthropist. Although, he has been a Canadian citizen, people always call him an American NRI. Now, he was engaged in social and developmental work. He has paid for the entire underground sewage system in the village, street lights, and a senior's home along with a health center. He has also revived the Kabbadi clubs in surrounding villages. This annual tournament has been organized to display his love for the favourite game of the Punjabis. Despite this glory, he still feared for his life. In the US, he was always guarded by gang members, but in

Punjab, Jagga has been protected by a security cover from the Punjab
police.

It was his villager and fellow American NRI, Kashmir Singh, who
secured police protection for Jagga. Kashmir Singh was a classmate
of Jagga. Unlike Jagga, Kashmir continued to study and finally found
work in the State Bank of India. His maternal uncle found an NRI
match for Kashmir in Sacramento, California. As Kahsmir Singh landed
in California, he joined his brother-in-law with his money exchange
business. The business was mainly focused on the Punjabi community
in California to send money through illegal channels to India, and bring
Indian Rupees in the US bypassing India's foreign currency exchange
laws. Every year tens of thousands of NRIs go back to India for holidays
or send money to their families in India for constructing homes or
buying assets like land. Most transactions by Punjabis abroad have been
performed by these money laundering networks. Money flow has been
in both directions. NRIs send money through these exchange networks
without the knowledge of Indian authorities at a higher exchange rate
than is offered by the banks. Indians also have access taking their money
out of India without state's approval or sanction but at a lower rate than
is offered by the banks. Most of the money coming out of India through
exchange networks is illegal or ill-gotten. A study estimated that the
annual out flow of this black money from India is between 11.6 billion
to 14.3 billion US dollars[12]. It provides a safety network to individuals
and their families who are engaged in the plunder of India through illegal
channels.

Kashmir Singh was quick to establish connections in India
through his friends from various branches of the state bank. Drug and
weapon smugglers, civil and police officials along with politicians and
businessmen of Punjab have accumulated large amounts of money through
illegal means. All over the world, the wealth accumulated through illegal
activities survives only with the help of money laundering operations
through both formal and informal networks. In a law-suit filed by the US
Justice Department, the HSBC has admitted laundering 881 million US
dollars for Mexican and Columbian drug cartels[13]. The HSBC, however,
is not the only bank involved in this dirty money laundering business.
Experts believe that the US law enforcement agencies track down and
seize no more than one per cent of the drug fortunes generated each
year by global cartels[14]. In this money laundering juggernaut, Kashmir

Singh's type of informal money exchange networks form only the tip of the iceberg. On a global scale, money is laundered for countless reasons. In Punjab, however, it is the fear of domestic law that allows income tax officials to investigate any individual who has 'accumulated assets disproportionate to his known sources of income'. In order to circumvent such laws, most people have found a way to transfer this ill-gotten wealth abroad. An NRI who required money in Punjab would deposit dollars with Kashmir Singh's exchange business in California, and within the hour, if not within minutes, the money would be delivered at doorsteps in Punjab. Since powerful individuals (civil and police officers or big businessmen and politicians) were in charge of delivering Rupees in India, there has never been any fear of law. Kashmir Singh's exchange matched Domino's pizza delivery claim by guaranteeing money delivery service in thirty minutes in any part of Punjab. The network through this money laundering business established by Kashmir also served to facilitate the settlement of Jagga in India. Jagga had also been useful to Kashmir in the initial years of his business. Kashmir had arrived in the US when Jagga was at the tail end of his jail sentence. Jagga could not forget that the only villager who had come to see him in jail was the newly settled Kashmir. Once Jagga established his network in California, he re-established relations with Kashmir. Jagga used this exchange to carry out transactions with Punjab based drug dealers. Kashmir also used Jagga for clients whose cheques bounced or who gave phony drafts. Jagga was also useful in 'eliminating' some of Kashmir's competition. Needless to say, both villagers were very close to each other.

On the tournament stage, both NRIs had introduced Amar Singh to all important organizers and guests. Amar Singh had received a large contribution from this group, thus he embraced each one of them with warm feelings. At the Kabbadi match's interval, Amar Singh was introduced to the spectators with glowing words as the next MLA of Dholpur and the cabinet minister of Punjab. The pumped-up Amar Singh made a long emotional speech. A section of the spectators started booing him but Jagga's muscle squad silenced them immediately. As a politician, Amar Singh had thick skin and did not pay much attention to his detractors. He praised both Kashmir Singh and Jagga as model citizens. He lauded their social work and commitment to the youth in the area. Like all other politicians, he also promised spectators and players to take Kabbadi to the summer Olympics. The Punjabi style Kabbadi has not even been recognized at India's national games, but that could not stop Amar Singh from offering the moon. He ended his speech with an appeal to ensure the Congress victory in the state and his victory in Dholpur. In the final moments of his speech, a scuffle broke out near the stage. The security apparatus was ready with their Ak-47s because most spectators were drunk by now. A villager was trying to convey a message to Amar Singh but he was stopped by members of the 'Youth Club'. The man in question was a Canadian NRI, Sewa Singh. The organizers assured Amar Singh that the scuffle was nothing more than a *Pagal* (mentally challenged) NRI's attempt to climb up to the stage.

Pagal Sewa Singh was also born and raised in this village. In his youth, he played field hockey and football at school and college levels. Like tens of thousands of other youth, Sewa's dream of finishing college education and finding a good government job ended with the rising violence and anarchy in the state. His parents pulled him out of college to save their only child from danger. A matrimonial advertisement from a Canadian NRI opened a new door for Sewa. He got married to an 'innocently divorced' Canadian woman 5 years older than him. It was only after he landed in Vancouver and started living a married man's life that he learned that his wife was not 'innocently divorced'. He used to dream how lucky and happy his wife's first husband must have been after the divorce. Life in a new country was not a bed of roses. He got a job in a lumber mill with the help of his father-in-law. Sewa's wife worked in a restaurant washing dishes. Despite their odd shifts, the couple had three children in two years. Twin boys and a girl meant that Sewa's wife could no longer work and he was now the only bread winner in the family. Instead of proper care for children in her free time, his wife spent most of her days watching Hollywood soap operas that she could not understand. Sewa wanted to sponsor his parents but his wife overruled such possibility. They both died waiting for Sewa's return in their native village. He was only able to attend the funeral of his mother who died just a few months after his father's death.

The first generation of immigrants must work hard to establish themselves in new lands, unless, of course, they are the likes of Jagga and Mike. Sewa was brought up with good moral values, and therefore, he wanted to accomplish everything in life through hard and honest work. He always remembered a story from Guru Nanak's life about honest living. According to Sikh tradition, the first Guru of the Sikhs, Nanak, was invited by a rich landlord, *Bhago*, to dine at his house. Guru Nanak refused the invitation by declaring that he smelled the blood of innocent peasants in the food of the landlord. The Guru, however, decided to dine at the house of a poor carpenter, *Lalo*, whose food he compared with sweet milk because it was earned through honest labour. As a true Sikh, Sewa truly believed in Guru's message. He was a hard worker who had never refused his supervisor's offer of working over-time. He also drove a taxi over the weekends to supplement his income. As a result, he had no time for his family. He was happy that he did not have to stay home with his wife, but sad that he could not spare time as his children were growing up. Sewa's wife could not comprehend the challenges facing the second generation of immigrants growing up in an environment of crony capitalism. Everybody was talking about money in the community and wealth was considered the only marker of success. Sewa's children grew up in an environment with dreams of riches but without any real capacity to earn a living. Although he had suspicions, he did not learn about his children's drug addiction until a tragedy hit the family. His daughter did not wake up from an overdose of cocaine. She was only in grade eleven and an angel to Sewa. He had almost no communication with his wife and boys, but he always thought he was closer to his daughter. Soon thereafter, Sewa learned that his boys had not only dropped out of high school to join a Punjabi drug gang, but were also addicted to drugs.

Sewa tried to speak with his sons about the dangers of gang life because he had witnessed the deaths of many young boys of Punjabi community. The communication gap between father and sons, however, had grown so wide that they hardly paid any attention to his advice. On the positive side, Sewa's wife started communicating with him to save their sons. The sons did not want to be bothered and moved out of the family house. Sewa and his depressed wife started living alone in a mega house they had built for their children. They woke up one weekend morning with a police knock on their door to hear the most tragic news for any parent- their son was shot dead by the rival gang. Only two weeks after the funeral, Sewa's wife died of a heart attack. During this period of massive grief, his only surviving son came home and stayed with Sewa. Unable to perform any work, Sewa took leave from his work. Although grief-stricken, he saw a ray of light as his son told him that he would like to lead a life without gangs and drugs. Father and son started living like a family once again but even this moment did not last long. One evening,

Sewa returned from a trip to the grocery store to see police cars parked all over the street. For the moment he thought his world had ended. His son was lying dead beside his sports utility vehicle. Immigrant Sewa Singh's journey to realize the Canadian dream ended with the funeral of the last surviving member of his family.

He sold his property in Canada, and came back to his ancestral village only to find out that his cousin had taken over his land and house. A kind neighbour gave shelter to Sewa. He was hoping Sewa would share his Canadian wealth with him and he was not wrong. Depressed and alone, Sewa kept to himself except on occasion when he would go out with his message: "Let's save our youth from drugs." He would repeat his message several times in a loud voice. The villagers started calling him *Pagal*. Now at the tournament, the youth club thrashed Sewa for repeating his *Pagal* message. He was not attempting to get on the stage, but only to catch Amar Singh's attention with his message, and he was hoping that the Congress candidate would also deliver the same message. The drug money's muscle power ensured no such message could be delivered at this sports tournament. Amar Singh was in a hurry to leave the grounds to resume his late evening campaign after the prize distribution. As he left the grounds, the organizers quickly moved crowds out of the grounds for fear of any violence. Members of the Youth Club had to mobilize volunteers for tomorrow's big event- Jagir Singh's long march. In the final days of the campaign, the Akali candidate wanted to display his political strength by passing through all 107 villages and 4 towns of the Dholpur constituency. This large village was selected as one of the seven sights for a full rally during the long march.

References

1. Kabbadi is a very intense and vigorously played Punjabi sport (a kind of combination between English Rugby and Greco-Roman style Wrestling).
2. The Ministry of Overseas Indian Affairs figures indicate that there are twenty million Indians abroad. See http://MOIA.Gov.In
3. Chinmay Tumbe (2012). "EU-India Bilateral Remittance." Working Paper Number 360, Banglore: Indian Institute of Management, p. 9.
4. *The Economic Times*, October 15, 2012.
5. Chinmay Tumbe (2012). op. cit., p. 9.
6. *Ibid.*

7.   An Indian proverb.

8.   For a full story of the Sikh secessionist movement, see my book *Sikh Ethnonationalism and the Political Economy of the Punjab*, New Delhi: Oxford University Press.

9.   Shinder Purewal (2012). "The Evolution of Sikh Secessionist Movement in Western Liberal Democracies." *International Journal of Business and Social Science*, Vol. 3 (18), p. 107.

10.   *Ibid.*, p. 110.

11.   An Indian proverb.

12.   Dev Kar (2011). "An Empirical Study on the Transfer of Black Money from India: 1948-2008". *Economic and Political Weekly,* Vol. 46 (15), p. 45.

13.   Robert Mazur, "How to Halt the Terrorist Money Train," in http://www.nytimes.com/2013/01/03/opinion/how-bankers-help-drug-traffickers-and-terrorists.html. Retrieved 4 January 2013.

14.   *Ibid.*

7

The Long March

God is on the side of the biggest battalion

— Napoleon

In *The Art of War*, Sun Tzu writes that "whoever is first in the field and awaits the coming of the enemy, will be fresh for the fight; whoever is second in the field and has to hasten to the battle, will arrive exhausted."[1] The Akali Dal had fielded almost all its candidates in the state well before the Congress even had a chance to review candidate's applications. The Congress high command in Delhi approved candidates only at the last moment just before the deadline to file nominations with the Election Commission. As an incumbent, Jagir Singh had the advantage to begin his campaign several months before Amar Singh who had only three weeks to campaign before the election day of January 30, 2012. Needless to say, Jagir Singh was ready and awaiting for Amar Singh in the field. 'If you are in a hurry', says a Chinese proverb, 'you will not get there'. The race had begun a long time back, and in haste, Amar Singh had made several mistakes including the weakness on the media front. The Congress party itself was unable to deal with the fallout from the nomination process. Once the party denied nominations, many disgruntled Congress hopefuls decided to contest the elections on an independent platform with a clear intention of defeating the official party candidate. They were encouraged and helped by the opposition Akali Dal and the BJP. Some were even encouraged by state Congress leaders to weaken their rivals within the party. In the words of Sun Tzu, the Akali Dal was provided "the opportunity of defeating the enemy... by the enemy himself."[2]

Jagir Singh wanted to enter the final phase of the campaign with a bang. After careful planning, the Akali campaign team had finalized the long march to cover all 107 villages and 4 urban centers of the Dholpur constituency. In order to avoid traffic jams on narrow link roads in the villages, the organizers decided to lead the march with youth mounted on motorcycles. The only four wheeler allowed in the march was Jagir Singh's SUV. The majority of the motorcyclists belonged to a powerful drug cartel of the state. They were the foot soldiers of Mumbai-based gangster Bhima. A major portion of the drug and weapons trade via the Indo-Pakistani border was controlled by the Bhima cartel. Historically, the Indo-Pakistan border has always been the source of smuggling, but it flourished during the Afghan war[3] as drug production and distribution increased many fold. India is surrounding by two great sources of drug production and smuggling: the Golden Triangle of Burma, Thailand Laos in the East, and the Golden Crescent of Iran, Afghanistan, and Pakistan in the West. The profits in drug trade are higher than those in oil and second only to those in the weapons trade[4]. As an open society with major international air routes, India has, according to a United Nations report, become a hub for the transport of heroin originating from the Golden Crescent to the rest of the world[5]. An alliance of Afghan-Pakistani and Indian drug dealers move heroin across the Indo-Pakistani border where it is handed over to Nigerian and Kenyan syndicates for international distribution. A study points out that the New Delhi-Lagos-Addis Ababa and the Mumbai-Lagos-Addis Ababa air routes are the favourites of these syndicates[6]. Not all drugs entering India leave its borders. Needless to say, a great portion of the drugs is distributed in the border regions of India for local consumption.

India is the largest producer of legal opium for pharmaceutical industries in the world, and Afghanistan is the largest producer of illegal opium in the world that is used to make heroin, which is more potent and easier to smuggle. Since 70 per cent of drugs enter India through land borders, Punjab's Lahore-Fazilka and Attari-Wagah borders have become major sources of drug trade[7]. It is estimated that roughly 60 per cent of all illicit drugs confiscated in India are seized in Punjab[8]. The drug cartels and syndicates of the region have also developed networks with terrorist movements, and, as a result, they are also engaged in illegal weapons trade. In India, this narco-terror nexus has extended its network to government officials and politicians. Alarmed at the strengthening of criminal-politician nexus, the government of India established a committee headed by the former home secretary Vohra to investigate this dangerous trend. The central government's own agency CBI (Central Bureau of Investigation), admitted in its submission to the

Vohra Committee that the criminals were not only funding politicians but also that many had entered politics to safeguard their interests. The director of CBI stated that:

> An organized crime syndicate/mafia generally commences its activities by indulging in petty crime at a local level....In port towns, their activities involve smuggling and the sale of imported goods and progressively graduate to narcotics and drug trafficking....Over time, the money power thus acquired is used for building up contacts with bureaucrats and politicians and expansion of activity with impunity. The money power is used to develop a network of muscle power which is also used by the politicians during elections[9].

The Intelligence Bureau (IB) of India, in its report to the Vohra Committee, added that:

> The cost of contesting elections has thrown the politicians into the lap of the criminal elements....There has been a rapid spread and growth of criminal gangs, armed *Senas*, drug mafias, smuggling gangs, drug peddlers and economic lobbies in the country, which have over the years, developed an extensive network of contacts with government functionaries....Some political leaders become the leaders of these gangs/armed *Senas* and over the years get themselves elected to local bodies, state assemblies, and the national parliament. Resultantly, such elements have acquired considerable political clout seriously jeopardizing the smooth functioning of the administration and the safety of life and property of the common man, causing a sense of despair and alienation among the people[10].

Despite these dire warnings from the state's key agencies, the criminalization of Indian politics has continued to date. At present, out of 776 Members of Parliament of both chambers and 4120 state legislators, some 1448, or 31 per cent of the total law makers of India, have criminal cases pending against them[11]. These criminal cases include rape, murder, attempted murder, kidnapping, robberies, extortion etc. In the current election in Punjab, all parties have fielded candidates with criminal cases pending against them in the judicial branch. A total of sixty one candidates have criminal cases with the Congress leading the pack with twenty-three per cent of its candidates, the Akali Dal with eighteen per cent, the BSP with fifteen per cent, and the PPP with eight per cent[12].

Further, the criminal element plays an active and sometimes a decisive role in the election of almost all state legislators and parliamentarians. Thus, the Akali candidate Jagir Singh was not alone in his reliance on the support of a drug smuggling gang. Almost all candidates from all major parties relied heavily on the support of drug, land, and liquor mafia for money and muscle power. Moreover, many mafia leaders were nominated by parties in assembly and parliamentary elections. Gangster Bhima, however, had no such political ambitions. It did not, however, mean that Bhima had no political connections. Both of his daughters were married in the families of top political leaders and his son was married to the daughter of a senior police officer of the state. He supported several top level candidates from the Congress, the BJP, and the Akali Dal during assembly and parliamentary elections. It was difficult for mafia cartels to survive without the official support.

Before his debut in the criminal underworld, Bhima was a known wrestler. The youngest of five siblings in a family of farmers, he was a rare combination of physical strength, intellect, and an iron willpower even during his childhood. His family had named him Bahadur (brave), and he did not disappoint them. He had started winning wrestling medals during his school years. Based on his academic and sports record, Bhima was offered a hefty scholarship in a sports college known for its wrestling and weightlifting teams. It was here that he was named Bhima by his coach. Noticing Bahadur's physical strength and mental alertness, the wrestling coach started calling him Bhima after the legendary warrior of *Mahabharata* who apparently had the strength of eight thousand elephants. It was also here in this college that he and some of his classmates became closely acquainted with a property dealer. India's rental and lease laws did not favour the owners of private property. Thus, it was difficult to vacate the premises from tenants. The urban land mafia took advantage of these laws to buy properties far below the market rates, vacate them, and sell them at higher prices. The property dealer used the muscle power of the 'wrestling club' and, in turn, offered them an extravagant lifestyle. Although his teammates considered this satisfying, Bhima was not happy with the status quo. Bhima found another network of property dealers to become a partner with an equal share in the profits which he shared with his friends. This was just the beginning for the wrestling champion. Soon thereafter, he had his own group armed with illegally acquired weapons to provide muscle power. Private bankers hired his services to recover bad loans, and powerful individuals relied on his gang to settle scores with their adversaries.

Bhima's fortunes changed as he was invited to a regional wrestling meet in Lahore, Pakistan. He lost the match, but he was able to develop contacts that helped his business flourish. Upon his return, Bhima started working with some politicians to establish necessary contacts with Indian customs, the BSF (Border Security Force), and the Punjab Police to clear everything from the Indian side of the border. A network was established and the business expanded beyond borders. He started making frequent trips to Dubai to settle accounts and close business deals with his Pakistani counterparts. During these trips, Bhima met super Kings of the game from other parts of India, especially Mumbai. These contacts proved helpful as the state of Punjab came into the grips of secessionist insurgency. On the Punjab and Kashmir borders, the drug and weapons trade was taken over by the Kashmiri and Sikh secessionists "to finance their operations"[13]. Bhima moved to Mumbai and continued his smuggling operations from other ports of India. After the return to normalcy in Punjab, he was the first one to develop motorcycle gangs to control the drugs and weapons trade along with kidnappings and robberies.

The operations of various motorcycle gangs have turned Punjab into a wild west. In the evening hours, these gangs move to occupy key junctions on all village link roads and on the outskirts of urban centers. Backed by law makers and law enforcement agencies, the gangsters rob with impunity. As a result, the state of Punjab has now become more dangerous than in the days of insurgency. For Bhima and other members of drug cartels, the business had never been better. In fact, the 'normal' life of Punjab has been great for the drug trade. The drug cartels have joined many social activists, politicians, writers, singers, and journalists to demand open border policy with Pakistan to encourage more trade. The language had been couched in terms of Indo-Pakistani friendship but the intent was always to open the flood gates to drugs coming from the Golden Crescent. Bhima had financed various peace conferences, or what were known as people to people contacts, through his politician relatives. He had even encouraged his gang members to help lead candle light vigils on the Indo-Pak border to promote inter-cultural friendship and peace.

The long march of the Akali candidate Jagir Singh, however, was no candle light vigil but a show of strength. More than 200 motorcyclists with saffron turbans and saffron flags of both the Akali Dal and the BJP were ready to deliver the message: Five more years of the Saffron Brigade. In view of restrictions imposed on larger convoys by the Election Commission, the motorcycle gang was divided into several platoons of 25 to 30 members. They were given different routes to march in the entire constituency and told to meet at the last rally of the day. The long march began with an early morning rally in the main urban centre of Dholpur. Jagir Singh was joined by a state level BJP leader, Ashok Tripathi. In a normal Punjabi fashion, every individual sitting on the stage was a speaker. The Akali-BJP city councillors were first to speak, followed by constituency level party leaders, then social and political activists, and finally, of course, Jagir Singh and Ashok Tripathi. The Master of Ceremonies urged all speakers to limit their speeches to two minutes. However, no speaker paid any attention including the MC himself who took more time than all the speakers combined. By the time both main speakers arose to speak, everything had been said about the Akali Dal and the BJP manifestos. Ignoring what had been said before him, Jagir Singh opened his remarks with two major messages of the Akali Dal: The Congress party has always been an enemy of the Sikhs and the Central government has always discriminated against the state of Punjab. He spoke about the *Atta-Dal* scheme for the poor including providing bicycles and lap-tops for students in secondary schools. Even in a purely urban area, he did not fail to mention that it was the Akali Dal which had provided a free power supply to farmers.

Finally, it was the BJP leader Ashok Tripathi's turn to rouse the masses. The people had shown remarkable levels of patience for the past two hours as speaker after speaker bored them with terrible speeches. Tripathi was a good orator and presented himself as a humble man. As a Brahmin, he had earned religious and social credentials by opening a *Gau Shala* (cow shelter) before entering active politics. The respect and reverence for the cow in Indian society has not been without reason. In what was a largely agricultural economy for centuries, the cow was not only a great source of milk and milk products but also of the bull, the greatest productive force, along with humans, for agriculture. In modern times, however, farm machinery has replaced the bull. Needless to say, the male offspring of the cow has become obsolete. Except for the milk cow, all other offspring of this animal have been abandoned by the people. As stray animals, they cause considerable damage to standing crops in India. As a result, the traders catch them and sell them to slaughter houses. This practice offends people's religious and cultural sensibilities. In opening a *Gau Shala*, Tripathi had continued an ancient tradition and earned people's respect. Now, there were rumours that a secret investigation was underway about the true nature of Tripathi's religious activities. Although he collects *Lakhs* of Rupees for this great charity, he has also turned *Gau Shala* into a dairy farm. Only the milk cows found shelter at the *Gau Shala* while others were deliberately left out at night for traders from the slaughterhouses. In a strange fashion, he was milking the charity from both sides.

On a more secular front, Tripathi was facing charges for misappropriating funds issued for urban development projects by state and central government. Regardless of investigative agency reports, the common defence of every politician and official is the claim of 'innocent until proven guilty.' The slow and corrupt wheels of Indian judiciary take years to find them 'not guilty.' Tripathi was a popular man in his urban constituency. He attended all religious and social functions in his area-birthdays and anniversaries, weddings and funerals. Further, he had a reputation of being accessible. Any member of the constituency was able to knock on his door even at midnight for any kind of assistance. In his speech, Tripathi mentioned how the Akali and BJP leaders were from the ranks of *Aam Janata* (common people) and therefore accessible to *Aam Admi* (the common people) compared with the Congress leadership. The target was Maharaja Amarinder Singh, the Congress chief, who was known for his inaccessibility not only to ordinary people but also to Congress legislators. Dwelling on the BJP manifesto for Punjab, Tripathi promised an Ombudsman's office in the state to investigate public complaints against those who held public office. He also spoke about his party's program to control inflation, albeit without any details. Noticing that the Akali candidate had only talked about the agricultural sector, Tripathi spoke about helping industry and trade sectors in the state to compete at national and international levels. Taking an indirect shot at India's neighbour, he promised to provide 'rehabilitation and settlement assistance to Hindu and Sikh families' forced to leave Pakistan[14].

As the speeches ended, the organizers found that even by Indian Standard Time the march was late. The motorcyclists were asked to move and lead the march through villages to the point of the next rally at Jagga's village. In this chaotic moment, a group of four young men requested a meeting with Jagir Singh. The leader of this group, Raj Kumar Singh Khushwaha or Roger had earlier spoken with Mohan regarding their work with high technology gadgets to help this campaign. He was asked to sit with Jagir Singh's grandson, Ajay Singh, in the back seat of an SUV to explain what he had on his mind. They had travelled from Delhi to sell an idea to parties and candidates to reach out to voters with email and text messages on mobile phones. Somehow they had an idea that such technology existed only in the metro cities. The '*Pendus*' (villagers), they thought, in Punjab would be thrilled to know their plan of reaching tens of thousands of voters in seconds. The group was part of a new class of NIR (Non-Indian Residents). Since the liberalization of the economy in the early 1990s, a class of English speakers and brand conscious Indians has developed in major urban centers. These sons and daughters of the *nouveau* rich either work, or aspire to work, in American call centers, and other franchises of the foreign multinationals. The NIR mind-set has a romanticized vision of North American and Western European life based on watching Baywatch and other Hollywood productions. When the British introduced the modern education system in India, Lord Macaulay wanted to produce a class of people who would be Indian in blood, but British in taste, opinion, morals, and intellect. Dr. Manmohan Singh's liberalization has produced a class of people who are Indian in blood, but American in taste and opinion[15]. While NRIs live abroad with India in their hearts, the NIRs live in India with America in their hearts.

Only God knows what happened; Ajay Singh kicked Roger out of the SUV in just two minutes. In the meantime, the caravan marched on to the venue of the next rally. People had already gathered in large numbers. Apart from being served *Chaa* and *Pakoras* (tea and fritters), they were entertained by a rustic Punjabi singer known for his gang-culture songs. As the election team arrived, Jagir Singh was joined on stage by a member of the SGPC, Inder Singh. The focus of Inder Singh's speech was largely to inspire Sikh youth to keep unshorn hair and take *Amrit* (baptization). In his early years, Inder Singh was a petty thief in his urban hometown. He used to steal car parts and sell them to a neighbour's auto body workshop. Although uneducated, he had a sharp mind. A jail sentence for assault with a deadly weapon opened the doors of politics for Inder. He met a major Akali leader of the area serving sentence for a second degree murder. Once out of jail, the Akali leader took Inder under his political command. They both started a profitable venture to do *Kar Seva* (religious volunteer service) in unknown historic Sikh temples. Hard working faithful Sikhs never questioned this money making venture. Most were blindly donating as much as possible to secure a place in heaven after death. In addition to this business, Inder's role was also crucial in forming political strategy and tactics. An incident in a local Gurdwara raised the community's tempers because the priest found several cigarette packs on temple premises[16]. Inder's mentor wanted to blame it on the Hindu *Suraksha Dal* (Protection Force), but they refused to take any responsibility and, in fact, condemned the incident. The Akali leader was not happy that no clashes took place between the two communities. Through his connections, Inder managed to get a cow's tail and threw it in *Shiv Mandir* (Temple of Shiva). For his mentor, the task was accomplished. The zealots came out on the streets, a curfew was imposed, and leaders from both communities were meeting civil and police officials. Such tactics made Inder the darling of hard line Akalis. He wanted the Akali Dal's nomination for an MLA seat, but the party managed to convince him to run for the SGPC. He accepted the party's offer and won his seat with a big margin.

As with the previous rally, Inder Singh, the MC, and other speakers took the lion's share of the time. Jagir Singh cut short his speech to move to the next rally. The next rally was at the village of *Dalit* Sarpanch. Party factionalism came to the fore because Sarpanch insisted that he would present the demands and introduce the candidate. The supporters of the Dhillon brothers, however, countered that the real village head was his wife and she should speak. After a huge debate, it was decided that one of the village elders would present the demands and Sarpanch would introduce Jagir Singh on the stage. Lachman Singh, an old Akali worker, was requested to present the demands to Jagir Singh in a short speech. He was an old supporter of the party who had courted arrests during the Punjabi suba movement and when he opposed Indira Gandhi's emergency rule. Everyone from Sarpanch's side told him to praise Jagir Singh for his development work in this area, but Lachman Singh was formed in the school of hard work and honesty. He stood up and started addressing the rally by first turning to Jagir Singh: "*Sardar Sahib*, we are a cluster of seven villages. From ancient times, people have referred to this area as the land of seven sisters. Our large village is the big sister (he laughed). I was asked to present some demands from this area, and I would like to thank you for coming and listening to us. First and foremost, the education facilities are almost non-existent. We have four elementary schools and only five teachers in all seven villages. There is only one secondary school, which is located in our village. The school is running without a headmaster and only a handful of teachers who are absent most of the time. A few decades back, we had a functioning health clinic with a doctor and a few nurses. We used to pay 10 *Paisa* (cents) to see the doctor and get free medicine. Now, a doctor or a nurse come once or twice a month to this collapsing building only to sell government medicine to a local chemist's shop. The streets of the village need pavement as all the water is collected in puddles. In all our lives, we walked freely in our area going from village to village. Sardar Sahib, the motorcycle gangsters now rule the link roads. We have complained to the police, but no action was taken against these robbers." Lachman Singh had said too much for the taste of Jagir Singh. His speech was abruptly interrupted to 'save time' for other speakers.

Finally, it was Jagir Singh's turn to address the gathering. As usual, the faithful started chanting slogans to please the candidate: "Long live Akali Dal! Long live BJP! Long live Sardar Parkash Singh Badal! Long Live Sardar Jagir Singh! Down with the Congress party! Jagir Singh encouraged slogan shouting youth long enough to ensure people would forget Lachman Singh's speech. He began his address by thanking everyone. "We have always fought with our opponents in the Congress party to give free electricity to farmers and *Dalits*," said Jagir Singh, as he started listing the achievements of the Akali-BJP government. "Only last year, we gave money to this village to make a paved road leading to your main *Gurdwara*. We also gave ₹ 2 Lakh to repair your ancient *Manair.* I remember only about 6 months back, we gave ₹ 50,000 to the youth clubs of this area. We gave ₹ 2 *Lakh* to our *Dalit* sister Sarpanch of this village for developmental work. I have just learned that there is no burial place for our Muslim community in the area. I promise to give 2 acres from *Shamlat* (communal) land for graves to Muslims of this area". The main thrust of Jagir Singh's speech was to show how his party had taken a balanced approach to look after all religious and caste communities. Whether it was a mistake or generosity, Jagir Singh had promised two acres for burial grounds to the area's nine landless Muslim families.

Time was in short supply, thus Jagir Singh ordered all rally venues to reduce the list of speakers to just two or three prominent persons of the village or area. Campaigns and wars never advance as planned. There are always twists and turns. A new twist brought long-awaited news to Jagir Singh. Suddenly he had to make an important stop at a major Congress leader's house on the way to his next rally. Kishor Kumar, a lawyer by profession, had decided to leave the Congress party to join the Akali Dal. Jagir Singh's team had been working on his conversion for a long time and the time had finally arrived to pick the harvest. In Punjab, a custom had developed for the campaign rallies of all candidates from all major parties to present *Siropas* (Saffron Robes) to those who switch loyalty from one party to the other. Most of these turn-coats were ordinary voters. But this major Congress leader of the Dholpur constituency was a big catch for Jagir Singh's campaign. His departure from the Congress personified Amar Singh's weakening campaign. A prominent Congress leader had already decided to run as an Independent after losing the battle for party nomination. "One cartload of enemy's provisions is equivalent to twenty of one's own," said Sun Tzu[17]. Jagir Singh understood the value of these numbers; thus the caravan was quickly diverted to Kishor Kumar's house despite the tight schedule.

Kishor Kumar was a one time student activist of the Congress affiliated National Student Union of India. His father had remained loyal to the Congress all his life and had contributed funds in every election. However, the father-son duo was never rewarded by the party for their loyalty. Kishor's father did not have much ambition and focussed instead on his rice Sheller business. He had also become a major Basmati exporter of the state. Kishor, on the other hand, had a law practice in the city and was an elected member of the Punjab and Haryana Bar Association. He held various constituency level and district level party posts, but Amar Singh lobbied hard to keep Kishor out of any patronage appointment by the state or central Congress governments. Unlike his father, Amar Singh had developed a practice of crushing his enemies within the party. The art of compromise was missing from his practices in dealing with opposition inside the party. 'You may lock up the rooster, but the sun will still rise'[18]. Amar Singh had suppressed numerous opponents within the Congress ranks, but opposition did not cease to exist. When you surround an enemy "leave an outlet free. Do not press a desperate foe too hard."[19] Amar Singh had pressed Kishor to the point of no other option than to leave the party. Jagir Singh's hawkish eyes were focused on Kishor for a long time, and during the campaign his emissaries worked hard to bring the Congress leader into the fold of the Akali Dal. Kishor was not only going to bring his key Congress supporters to Jagir Singh's campaign; he was also going to pose a serious problem to the PPP candidate's support in the Bania community.

As the caravan arrived, Kishor had managed a reasonably large crowd of supporters, *albeit* mainly the Sheller workers, to welcome Jagir Singh. The Akali candidate's communication advisor had asked the media team to quickly take photos and prepare a story for tomorrow's newspapers to highlight this desertion in the Congress ranks at the eleventh hour. After customary speeches amid joyous cheers, Jagir Singh took Kishor with him to attend rallies for the rest of the day. The final rally was organized in a large village close to the river. One of the Akali Dal's key state leaders was coming to address the rally, thus the standing orders from the campaign team were to move all supporters for a big show. This area had given Jagir Singh a major lead during the 2007 campaign. Although some of his support had shifted to the Congress, Jagir Singh still had an edge in these villages. A hotbed of major illicit liquor production had also become a center of drug production and distribution. Bhima's gang produced methamphetamine pills in a secret location close to the river. As the liquor production and distribution market got saturated and less profitable, the youth of this area became easy prey for drug distribution networks. While the profits of drug lords multiplied, the drug addiction levels reached unprecedented levels in the villages. Jagir Singh's caravan was now travelling through small villages on the river bank where drug addiction had reached its zenith. One village en route was simply known as widow's village. Most adult men of this village had died from drug addiction and the families were now headed by females. The fate of other villages of this corridor was not any better.

It was cold, dark, and foggy. Despite powerful lights, the venue of the rally had a very low visibility. Most addicts of the village and surrounding area were given free doses of drugs and bottles of alcohol to remain warm. India's election commissioner, Shahabuddin Yaqoob Quraishi noted with concern that "we have encountered the problem of liquor during election in almost all states....But drug abuse is unique only to Punjab"[20]. Free distribution of illicit drugs, along with liquor in Punjab, only showed the seriousness of drug addiction in the state. The ends justify the means in this land of five rivers. This rally itself was a means to occupy executive power in the state. The show of strength was to convince the weak minded swing voters who would vote for a likely winner. In the past two decades, the political polarization of the state had produced a vendetta politics. The party in power made it difficult for the supporters of the opposition to lead normal lives. Even at this rally, the Akali Dal's might was on full display. In the absence of a large police force, Jagir Singh's muscle squad was ready to maintain peace and order in this large gathering. All motorcycle parties had arrived for the final stop of the day. A senior Akali leader had come to address the rally to show people of this area how important Jagir Singh's seat was for the game of numbers in Punjab *Vidhan Sabha* (Assembly) elections.

Amar Singh, on the other hand, did not panic with the departure of Kishor Kumar and a successful long march of Jagir Singh. His party leaders in the state were convinced that the Congress would form the next government, and Amar Singh was convinced about his own victory in Dholpur. He had his own catch of the day-a BJP leader and former MLA from neighbouring constituency. It was done during the day time to counter Jagir Singh's headline in tomorrow's papers. Although the BJP ex-MLA was not from the constituency, and turned against his party only when denied the ticket, the symbolic value of his declaration of support to Amar Singh was of equal if not higher value than the departure of Kishor Kumar from the ranks of the Congress. Furthermore, Amar Singh was able to convince the BJP leader to join him on his door-to-door campaign in a major urban center of Dholpur. Although he was unable to match Jagir Singh's long march, Amar Singh declared that he did not believe in blocking traffic in the entire constituency to say good-bye to people in a road show. He told reporters that he would like to meet voters in their homes and businesses on a personal basis. A door-to-door campaign was his style.

References

1. Sun Tzu (2002). *The Art of War*. Meneola, New York: Dover Publications, translated by Lionel Giles, p. 58.
2. *Ibid.,* p. 52.
3. For a well-documented study linking Islamic warriors and the drug trade, see Gretchen Peters (2010). *Seeds of Terror: How Drugs, Thugs and Crime are Reshaping the Afghan War*. New York: Macmillan.
4. Ashish Shukla (2010). "Drug Trafficking in Pakistan: Threat to Regional Security." *Journal of Himalayan and Central Asian Studies*, Vol. 14 (3), p. 2.
5. Cited in Pushpa Das (2012). "Drug Trafficking in India: A Case of Border Security." Delhi: Institute for Defence Studies and Analysis (IDSA), Occasional Paper No. 24, p. 11.
6. *Ibid.,* pp. 16-17.
7. *Ibid.,* p. 13
8. http://www.nytimes.com/2012/04/19/world/asia/drugs-drug-addiction-is-a-growing-problem-in-punjab.html, Retrieved 24 December 2012.
9. "Vohra Committee Report" (1995). *The Indian Journal of Public Administration*, Vol. 41 (3), p. 641.
10. *Ibid.*, p. 642.
11. *The Times of India*, July 12, 2012.
12. Punjab Election Watch 2012 (2012). Delhi: A Report by the Association for Democratic Reform, p. 3.
13. Pushpa Das, op. cit., p. 5
14. BJP Manifesto: Punjab Assembly Election 2012, in *Outlook*, January 24, 2012.
15. The term Non-Indian Residents (NIR) was coined by Professor Jayant Kumar Lele of Queen's University, Canada.

16. The Sikh Code of Conduct strictly prohibits smoking tobacco or tobacco related products.
17. Sun Tzu (2002). op. cit.,p. 46.
18. An Indian proverb.
19. Sun Tzu (2002). op. cit.p. 68.
20. http://www.nytimes.com, op. cit.

8

Door-to-Door Campaign

You can fool some of the people all the time, and those are the ones you want to concentrate on

– George W. Bush

It is a great wonder of democracy that the most arrogant heads are lowered in a most humble fashion before the most ordinary people, at least once every five years. A door-to-door campaign gives citizens a sense of pride and, at the same time, a sense of humility to politicians. Direct personal contact also shows voters that a campaign is not an abstract phenomenon, but a living and breathing candidate with a campaign team. This personal approach builds confidence among people that in the next five years they will have someone to tend to their concerns. For a candidate, it's a great source of word of mouth communication, and a potential source of volunteers for the campaign. Amar Singh wanted to send a warm personal message to constituents in the final days of the campaign. A day later, he was a little uneasy over Jagir Singh's successful long march. As a result, he had to be more creative to overcome a sense of under achievement in a campaign where his own party had held him back. His campaign team showed cleverness in opting for smaller meetings in neighbourhoods instead of knocking on each and every door in the presence of some hostile media. Unlike villagers, the urban residents do not feel obligated to open their doors for everyone, and unlike the stray dogs roaming the streets of villages, the urban dogs are kept as pets inside the homes and they bark at every knock to the door. Many candidates have found this experience humiliating, and Amar Singh's team showed much wisdom in avoiding such negative perceptions.

The first stop for Amar Singh and his team was an early morning gathering at gynecologist Jagdev Singh Kohli's ancestral residence.

Dr. Kohli lived in the state capital of Chandigarh with his wife and two sons. He came back to the town of his birth for three days to help his business partner, Amar Singh, and to visit his parents who continued to live in the family home. For the past two decades, Dr. Kohli had focused on the booming business of private health care. In a carefully drafted business strategy, he has maintained a majority ownership of fifty-one per cent in all ventures. Some key political figures of the state, as well as officials from police and civil services, were shareholders in the remaining forty-nine per cent. The majority of their profits have been generated from the booming business from Dr. Kohli's own profession of gynecology. In almost all major cities of the state, they have gynecology clinics with the most sophisticated technology to kill female fetuses. For centuries, women of India, along with the *Dalit*s, have borne the brunt of barbaric socio-economic oppression. In the words of a great Indian reformer, Ram Mohan Roy:

> "What misery do the women not suffer? At marriage the wife is recognized as half of her husband, but in after conduct they are treated worse than inferior animals. For the woman is employed to do the work of a slave in the house, such as in her turn to clean the place very early in the morning, whether cold or wet, to scour the dishes, to wash the floor, to cook night and day, to prepare and serve food for her husband, father and mother-in-law, sister-in-law, brother-in-law, and friends and connections....If in the preparation and serving up the victuals they commit the smallest fault, what insult do they not receive from their husband, their mother-in-law...."[1]

Women were first to rise in the morning and last to sleep at night; they were first to cook and last to eat. Indian society, in general, and Punjabi society, in particular, has always recorded the highest child mortality rate for female children. In addition, the denial of education in childhood, the demands of dowry and dowry related deaths, rapes and humiliations have haunted the female gender whatever life has had in store for individual women. In medieval India, after the death of their husbands, women were expected to either live like ascetics or to commit *Sati* (the burning of the female on her husband's funeral pyre). In traditional society, women faced death after they were born, but in a technologically advanced society of the 21st century, they face abortion months after conception in the womb of their mothers. It was this female foeticide that made the likes of Dr. Kohli rich beyond dreams.

Anderson and Rey's study of 'missing women' in India concluded that if women were not subject to unnatural deaths, there could potentially be 25 million more women alive today[2]. Nobel Laureate Amartya Sen, who coined the term 'missing women', claimed that the actual number was 100 million if one were to include inequality and neglect leading to excess female mortality[3]. As the amniocentesis and ultrasonography technologies have expanded, the per centage of the females in population has continued to decline. The first gender-determination clinic was opened in the holy city of Amritsar in 1979, and now they have mushroomed everywhere in Punjab. Despite the passing of laws like the one relating to Pre-Natal Diagnostic Techniques (Regulation and Prevention of Misuse), the government has been unable, or unwilling, to stop this genocide. Compared with the rest of India, the state of Punjab has recorded the second lowest female to male ratio after Haryana. In the decennial census of 2011, it was revealed that in the age group of zero to six, there were only 846 females per thousand males in the state of Punjab[4]. In rural areas, there were only 843 females per thousand males and 851 females per thousand boys in the urban centers[5]. Despite widespread knowledge of female foeticide in the state, not a single person was arrested in 2011 under the Pre-Natal Diagnostic Techniques Act[6]. When the Act was first created in 1994, the government of India had been dragging its feet for not promulgating it. It was under such intense public pressure that the government finally decided to implement the Act and create regulations to enforce it. The practical results of this 'enforcement' are still missing like the 'missing women' of India.

Dr. Kohli's gynecology clinics follow a set pattern in this murderous business. Each clinic hangs a board in the front with the following message: 'Gender determination tests are not conducted in this clinic.' This is a code word to inform potential customers that such tests are actually available in the clinic. The technology was meant for detecting any abnormality in the unborn child, but it has now mainly focused on the gender determination process. Once a test determines the gender of the fetus, it is normally "followed by sex-selective abortion."[7] Most of such abortions have never been recorded. The untold numbers of aborted female fetuses end up in the urban sewers of India. While these clinics have become the graveyards of unborn females, the same clinics have new technology to provide boys to couples. The uneducated still continue to visit the *Deras* of *Baba*s, while the educated rely more on modern technology. Dr. Kohli's clinic has claimed that with new technology, they can separate X and Y chromosomes. The process enables them to fertilize the female egg with Y chromosome to produce a baby boy. This happens in a society that worships females in the form of *Durga* (goddess of power), *Sarswati* (goddess of knowledge) and *Laxami* (goddess of wealth). Declaring that women are equal to men in every sense of the word, Guru Nanak wrote that 'other than God, it is female who gives birth to new life'. According to a Punjabi proverb, 'blessed is a woman, whose first born is a baby girl'[8].

Yet, the status of women in almost all traditional societies has left much to be desired. The process of economic, social, and political modernisation, however, has enhanced the role and status of women, albeit to a point that is still short of equality. The wheel of modernization in India has moved with force, but the mindset regarding women remains stuck in medieval times. Even in the domain of electoral politics, women of India have made very little headway. India's first parliament had 4.4 per cent women in Lok Sabha (lower chamber of parliament). At present, women in the 15th parliament represent only 10.8 per cent of the total elected body[9]. The average representation of women in all parliaments of the world is only 19.3 per cent[10]. Even by the standard of this low level of representation worldwide, India stands at the lowest end of the spectrum. In the current election in Punjab, political parties have only fielded 7 per cent female candidates. Leading the pack was the Akali Dal with 12 per cent female candidates, followed by the BJP with 10 per cent, the Congress with 9 per cent, and the PPP with only 4 per cent[11]. A constitutional amendment bill to reserve one-third of parliamentary seats for women has been doing rounds for more than a decade without any results.

It was ironic that more women than men came to attend the meeting at Dr. Kohli's house. After the breakfast and hand shaking, Dr. Kohli introduced another Chandigarh resident to Amar Singh. Bobby was one of the key leaders of the Animal Rights Protection Group in Punjab. Amar Singh and Bobby moved to a small room for a short private meeting at Dr. Kohli's suggestion. Bobby was born and raised in this town and, much like Dr. Kohli, his parents and siblings continued to live here. His family had a religious business. Bobby's grandfather was a Sikh priest in the local *Gurdwara*. His father decided to open a small business to sell religious books and artifacts in the vicinity of the temple. Bobby and his siblings were raised in a comfortable middle class environment, but the family's low caste status always haunted Bobby. They were followers of a religion that denounced the traditional Indian caste system in theory. In practice, however, nothing had changed in centuries. During his high school and college days, Bobby developed close friendships with activists of the BJP affiliated *Akhil Bhartya Vidyarthi Parishad* (All-India Student Association). He had a clever mind and a desire to become an important man. He was looking for fame and money but did not have the courage to do something 'openly' illegal. A few small ideas helped his father's business. He suggested that his father should also keep Hindu religious books and artifacts to double the customer base. The idea worked and his father was impressed with Bobby's mental sharpness.

After college, Bobby and his close friends started focusing on religious funds for festivals and on the construction and repair of Hindu-Sikh shrines. There was nothing legal or illegal about this holy activity because fund raising companies were allowed to keep portions of charitable donations. The moral or ethical side of this business did not bother them because they were partially helping god. What got them in trouble was a big fund raising opportunity to settle Hindu families who were forced to leave their ancestral homes in villages and towns of Kashmir by gun-toting terrorists. Sympathetic people showed generosity by contributing to this fund, and Bobby and his friends showed their moral degradation by embezzling the funds. They were all expelled from this fundraising activity. As the story appeared in the local newspaper, the *Gurdwara* management summoned Bobby's grandfather for a meeting. Bobby accompanied his grandfather to the meeting and vigorously defended his conduct. He told the management that he was expelled by this Hindu organisation because he was a baptized Sikh. The management accepted his explanation and ended the meeting by condemning Hindu chauvinism. No one questioned the fact that four of his Hindu friends were also expelled.

Bobby changed his course and joined a Human Rights organisation. He was told by a friend that human rights were popular throughout the western world and there were opportunities to visit western capitals to attend conferences. In anticipation of foreign travel, Bobby became a clean shaven gentleman. On the anniversary of a major fake police encounter in the city, the human rights activists decided to hold a rally demanding action against police officials who had killed a young man under dubious circumstances. Two days later, a local police inspector arrested Bobby in connection with an ongoing case of a jewellery store robbery. One night in a police station ended Bobby's association with human rights group forever. Now this sharp mind had become a major liability for the family. Bobby's father spoke with a relative in Chandigarh and asked Bobby to move and find some work in the state's capital. It was here in Chandigarh that Bobby got involved with the Animal Rights group and fulfilled his desire to be an important person. How he got involved with the national group was a different story. His friends thought it was his pursuit of a pretty girl in the Animal Rights group, but Bobby narrated a more moving story. One of his neighbours would beat his dog on a regular basis for no reason. Bobby intervened and rescued the dog. He had a philosophic awakening to the plight of animals unable to convey their feelings of hurt and neglect at the hands of humans.

As he moved up the ladder in the Animal Rights group, Bobby started using his position and connections to build a more financially secure future. Thanks to the lobbying of this group, the government has banned most animal related sports. The landlords of Punjab could no longer have their greyhound races with live rabbits, and the farmers could no longer have bullock cart races in festivals. In close association with the police, Bobby and his friends would turn a blind eye to greyhound races. Laws related to the cruelty of animals became sources of blackmail and money making venture for Bobby and friends. As a leader of the Animal Rights group, Bobby managed to get twenty four hour police protection. People in high society started taking his advice as he became a master of Machiavellian tactics. Just recently, he had helped the leader of a Hindu organisation to get police protection. It has become a matter of prestige and honour to be guarded by police or para-military forces in Punjab. The need to provide such security to politicians, government officials, and important leaders in society arose from the days of Sikh insurgency. Two decades after the end of the insurgency, the leaders of Punjab have not given their security covers. It's not surprising to note that ten per cent of the total Punjab police force was devoted to these personal security duties. Thus, anyone who considered himself a leader knew that the public would not acknowledge his leadership without a police security cover. This Hindu leader was facing the same dilemma. Bobby managed a shoot-out at his residence when his family was in the temple for prayer and plastered his house walls with posters threatening to kill him. All this was done in the name of a Sikh secessionist group. Along with a huge bribery, this action was enough to convince Punjab police to provide security for this leader of a minor Hindu organisation.

Amar Singh was not too comfortable standing with Bobby in this room. During election, a politician must have the capacity to listen, even to the most outrageous ideas. Bobby had two such ideas. His first proposal was to call activists of the Animal Rights group in the area to stand with the Congress candidate for a photo endorsing Amar Singh's candidacy. A backlash of unpopularity flashed before Amar Singh's eyes by just listening to this idea. People in rural and urban centers have blamed the Animal Rights group for the growing population of stray dogs. Under pressure from this highly organised urban group of upper middle class activists, the government banned the old barbaric practice of annihilating stray dogs on a yearly basis. The state, however, never provided alternative way of controlling the population of stray dogs that have become a menace in rural and urban India. Each year, twenty thousand Indians die from dog bites, largely as a result of rabies[12]. In Punjab, the problem has worsened as a result of green revolution technologies. The old cycle of life has disappeared. The bodies of dead animals have always been disposed in open spaces outside the villages and towns. The village *Mochi* (shoe maker) would peel the skin of the animal and leave the meat for vultures. The vultures became extinct because their natural habitat of *Bohar* (Ficus Bengalines) trees had disappeared from the landscape of Punjab. The stray dogs have replaced the vultures in eating the meat of dead animals. A pack-mentality has developed among these dogs that stay in groups. As a result, incidents of dog bites have increased along with the spread of rabies. India accounts for one-third of the total rabies-related death toll in the world[13]. In the absence of dead animal meat, these dogs go after living animals and even humans. Children, the weak, and the elderly have been victimized. In 2011, there were more than fifteen thousand people bitten in Punjab by these dogs[14] and many were eaten alive. Since the victims were often from the poor segments of the population, the authorities could not be bothered to find a solution. Most people blamed all this on Animal Rights activists. Thus, Amar Singh had to politely decline Bobby's offer of support.

Bobby's second proposal disturbed Amar Singh the most. "We can arrange an attack on you," said Bobby. "The attack will involve few shots but not on any person; most bullets will hit the vehicle," he continued. "We can arrange this in the name of any Muslim terrorist group, but the Congress high command will not like it. Your party depends on Muslim support. The best would be a Sikh secessionist organisation. After this incident, a group will issue a press release on its letter pad and even make a call to a newspaper and a TV station....This will create sympathy not only for you but for the entire party. What do you think?" asked Bobby at the end of this conspiratorial proposal. Amar Singh was no stranger to the world of realpolitik, but he was stunned to hear such a proposal from a person he always considered a vagabond. Bobby had become a modern Chanakya[15], but Amar Singh had lost all his patience and walked out to attend the morning get-together of Dr. Kohli's neighbourhood. As he complained about this meeting with Bobby, the Doctor assured Amar Singh that he was a harmless fellow who would not utter a word to anyone else. Amar Singh knew that one must be 'careful of deep waters and dogs that do not bark'[16]. It was time to forget about the past few minutes and move on with the neighbourhood meeting. Dr. Kohli introduced Amar Singh as a friend and a great public figure. Taking note of the heavy presence of women in the meeting, Amar Singh focused on the party's platform aimed at women voters. "Our party," said Amar Singh, "will give each family ₹ 15,000 on the occasion of the birth of a girl child. We have also announced a *Shagun* (wedding gift) scheme of ₹ 31,000 for women from poor families."[17] Women in this gathering of the middle and upper-middle class, however, were more interested in educational and job opportunities for their children. Amar Singh gave evasive political answers to all these serious questions, but he was caught by a surprise question from an older person on immoral activities in the city. A well-known female supporter of Amar Singh was caught in a controversy of operating prostitution business in the name of beauty parlours. "How can you help us in stopping this immoral activity in our neighbourhoods?" asked the woman in the audience. "We all know that there is no place for immoral and vulgar activities in our ancient culture," replied Amar Singh. "We all need to sit together as families to meet such challenges....We owe it to our younger generation that the moral and ethical environment must conform to our civilized standards....Together we can find a solution to any problem." As he quickly finished his remarks, he gave a call to mobilize support to assure his victory.

The next meeting was in a *Halwai's* (Traditional Cook) house where the BJP's ex-MLA had already gathered a crowd of prominent Hindu leaders of the town. The idea of walking to that house was abandoned as a result of last night's drizzle, which turned the street into piles of mud. As Amar Singh got out of Dr. Kohli's house to sit in his SUV, a group of Gandhian agitators from the 'India Against Corruption' (IAC) group greeted him with placards against the Congress government in Delhi. This movement was started in 1991 by a Gandhian leader from Maharashtra, Anna Hazare. Recently, he was joined by Indian's *Yoga* Guru-baba Ramdev. The basic demand of the group was to implement the rule of law so as to end corruption in India, in general, and to create an Ombudsman's office, in particular. Despite constitutional provisions, the rule of law did not apply equally to everyone. There are three distinct groups treated in three different ways by the law enforcement agencies of the state. The top group consists of politicians, civil, judicial, police, paramilitary, and military officials. This group's strength comes from its membership in the state and government institutions. Thus, they are generally above all laws. The second group belongs to businessmen, religious leaders, civil society leaders, and other power blocs from formal and informal sectors of the society. The power of this group comes from the economic sources and the sources of tradition in society. This group is also generally above the law so long as the group members are not targeted by the first group. The third group of more than a billion Indians is subject to all known and unknown laws of the land. Demanding one law for all, Anna Hazare agitated for the creation of an Ombudsman's office to investigate cases of corruption against public officials. The Congress led government in Delhi disagreed with the draft proposal of IAC, but formed an all-party parliamentary committee to formulate its own bill. The sturdy Anna Hazare, a former soldier of valiant Maratha Regiment, refused to go along with the government proposal and decided to go on a hunger strike. The Indian government celebrates the birth of *Rashterpita* (father of the nation) Mahatma Gandhi with fanfare every October 2, but refuses to allow Gandhian *Satygrah* in modern India. The strong arm tactics of the state backed by police action ended Anna Hazare's fast. As a result, the Congress party's handlers managed to turn public anger against corruption into public outrage against the Congress. Now, the Congress candidates were paying the price on the ground in the state assembly elections.

Halwai Shiv Kumar Bhatia's house was not very far. Amar Singh was welcomed with garlands by an enthusiastic crowd. Bhatia's house was bigger than most small town motels in North America. His father had started with a small sweet shop in this town. The business expanded rapidly to shops in other cities as well as gas agencies and petrol pumps obtained with political connections. The latest business for the Bhatia family was the creation of a college to dish out diplomas and degrees in the expanding private education sector of India. The expansion of the middle class opened opportunities in private schools and post-secondary institutions as the state changed its direction from public sector to private sector. Although the Bhatias knew very little about education, they had an eagle eye for business. The education sector provided a greater potential for windfall profits than other comparative investments. Bhatias, however, faced rivalry and competition from another business family of the area with closer ties to the BJP and the Akali Dal. They had successfully blocked Bhatia's attempt to convert this college into a full-fledged university. The BJP ex-MLA had brokered a deal between Bhatias and Amar Singh to lobby for a University status in the event of a Congress victory in the state assembly. Thus, in private, the Bhatia family had agreed to back Amar Singh with major financial donation as well as to contribute to the state level funds for the Congress coffers. As there were too many neighbourhood meetings planned for the day, Amar Singh quickly grabbed the opportunity to address the crowd. There was nothing special in the Congress manifesto to please this crowd of traders and shopkeepers. The speech thusly focused on the 'non-performance' of the Akali-BJP government. He also appealed to the religious emotions of the crowd by asserting the common bonds of Hinduism and Sikhism. He accused his opposition of creating violent insurgency in Punjab that created a wedge between two communities. "*Bhagawat Gita* states God's message in clear terms, 'only in love can men see me, and know me, and come unto me,'"[18] said this secular candidate. "A similar message is delivered by Shri Guru Gobind Singh Jee in *Dasam Granth*; 'only the one who is absorbed in true love shall attain the lord,'"[19] he concluded.

Feeling like a scholar, Amar Singh went from neighbourhood to neighbourhood addressing meetings. The last meeting of the day was organized in a poor *Mohalla* of *Dalit*s and migrant workers organised by a union leader. Comrade Kulwant Singh was a well-known trade unionist and a known Communist of this area. It was his activism in the ranks of the Communist Party of India-Marxist (CPM) that led him to lead a local chapter of the Centre of Indian Trade Unions (CITU) at a public undertaking. In the massive public sector, especially in heavy industries, the Indian state had established a tripartite labour relations system. The trade union representatives sit along with the management team and state bureaucrats on a round table to participate in the decision-making process. Along with CITU, other parties have their trade union bodies in such tripartite bodies: the Communist Party of India (CPI) affiliated All-India Trade Union Congress (AITUC), the BJP affiliated *Bhartya Mazdoor Sangh* (Indian Workers Association), and the Congress affiliated Indian National Trade Union Congress (INTUC). The tripartite system allows trade union leaders to share briberies with the management and civil servants. From time to time, however, the political affiliation of these trade unions puts them at loggerheads. The Communist affiliated unions worked extremely hard to maintain labour peace in the Communist ruled West Bengal and Kerala while the BJP and the Congress affiliated unions worked to cause labour unrest. On the other hand, the Communist led trade unions performed similar function in the BJP and Congress led states. Comrade Kulwant Singh knew about this fishy business but like most junior leaders of the trade union he remained silent.

In the absence of a Communist candidate, Kulwant decided to support the Congress candidate. He accused the Akali Dal and the BJP of playing communal politics in the state, and urged all 'progressive' voters to defeat them in the upcoming election. Comrade Kulwant had also criticized the Congress in the past for communalism and the politics of division, especially when the party promoted leaders involved in the 1984 Sikh massacres. During the Indo-US nuclear deal, he had blasted the role of 'US imperialism' and justified the party's decision to join hands with the BJP in an attempt to bring down the Congress government on a vote of non-confidence in Lok Sabha. In this election, both Communist parties had formed a political alliance with the Manpreet Singh Badal led PPP, but Kulwant had decided to support the Congress. "The primary contradiction is between communal and secular politics in Punjab," said Kulwant. "Thus, we must support the Congress to defeat communal parties." Whenever someone pointed out contradictions in his own opinions and statements, Kulwant knew how to justify himself by resorting to the classic ideas of Marxism-Leninism. His standard reply was: "Mao used to say that contradiction is inherent in everything."[20] Despite his contradictory positions, Kulwant was a popular man among the poor, *Dalit*s, and migrant workers. Thus, his endorsement was important for Amar Singh. By the time the Congress candidate was ready to speak, almost everyone attending the meeting was drunk with free liquor supplied by Amar Singh's camp. In order to prevent any unruly behaviour, Amar Singh's muscle brigade was ever ready.

In the last days of the campaign, Amar Singh was more worried about the BSP's campaign than his own. Conventional wisdom was that the BSP was taking away the old and solid support base of the Congress party among Dalit voters. Amar Singh had sent friendly gestures to the BSP candidate to slow-down his campaign. There were various offers on the table including cash. The campaign of the *Dalit* party, however, continued with vigour and energy. There were widespread rumours that the Akali candidate had funded the campaigns of the Congress independent and the BSP candidate. Unable to say anything regarding these rumours in public, Amar Singh reminded *Dalit* voters that it was the Congress that had appointed Bhim Rao Ambedkar to the powerful position of chair in the constitution draft committee. The Congress had supported and implemented reservations for *Dali*ts and *Adivasis* (tribal) in government jobs and in electoral politics. "In this election," said Amar Singh, "our party has decided to create ₹ 100 crore (one billion) venture capital fund to support enterprise by *Dali*ts."[21] He was speaking to a crowd of daily wage earners. Apart from Kulwant Singh's fiery speech in defence of workers' rights, the stage offered nothing to attract the attention of the *Dalit* and migrant workers. In fact, Kulwant had suggested two different rallies for this crowd because *Dalit* workers did not get along with migrant workers. *Dalits* often accused migrant workers of stealing their jobs and lowering the wages in Punjab. The Congress team had the view that all poor people had a group identity and, therefore, a sense of belonging.

The rally ended with slogan shouting, although no one could make out what the drunkards were saying. Before heading back to the campaign office, Amar Singh had to make a visit to an old freedom fighter's house in the town. Pandit Madan Lal was an old Congress leader from the days of Mahatma Gandhi. He had joined Gandhi's freedom movement as a teenager. As a result, Madan Lal was jailed by the British on several occasions during the days of the Raj, and by his own party during the period of emergency in independent India. At age 97, Madan Lal had seen the best and the worst in his country and among his people. He had witnessed millions of Indians rising to the occasion under the leadership of Gandhi to demand freedom, liberty, and independence. People faced *Lathis* (bamboo sticks) and bullets, prisons and gallows to demonstrate their audacious spirit to foreign rulers. Madan Lal had also witnessed the carnage related to the division of the sub-continent in 1947. People butchered each other in the name of religion to demonstrate the dark side of humanity. Despite torrents of blood, he saw new India emerging from the old with confidence and vision. The country's leadership demonstrated its ability to march on the high road of civilization in both its domestic and foreign policies. They had given a clarion call to millions of Indians from North to South, East to West, to focus all their energies on development and to make India a self-reliant, secular, and democratic nation. Now he was witnessing the degeneration of both the leaders and citizens. The clarion calls of today's leaders focus on creating divisions among people and defending the special privileges of the ruling elite. He was simply puzzled to witness the amount of corruption and the rising power of the criminal underworld. An optimistic and energetic Madan Lal was a sad man toward the end of his life. Like many other freedom fighters, he had a firm faith that the democratic system with the rule of law had the capacity, as the Greeks would say, to take the savage out of the man. Alas, the degeneration of the democratic process in India, in fact, had increased the savage in the man.

Amar Singh only stopped for a quick cup of warm milk at Madan Lal's house. He was in a rush to meet his team to finalize the strategy for the last hours of the campaign. Anything was possible in this tight race. Moreover, he was in no mood to hear Madan Lal's sermons about ethics and morality. While Amar Singh appreciated such advice during his free time, now the focus had to be on victory rather than ethics and morality. This soul searching journey was good for philosophers, he thought, but in the domain of electoral politics, one must repeat a lie thousand times to assure victory. Ethical and moral governance must remain confined to the promises of Manifestos. In practice, it was neither possible, nor desirable. Amar Singh was born and raised in the era of corruption and briberies. His family had built fortunes during this period. According to an Indian proverb 'a person blinded during the monsoon remembers only the colour green'. Thus, Amar Singh was neither able, nor willing, to imagine a society and government based on moral standards and ethical conduct. In a democracy, he thought, 'people get the government they deserve'[22].

References

1. *Second Conference between an Advocate for and an Opponent of the Practice of Burning Widows Alive*, Cited in *Sources of Indian Tradition*, Volume II, Edited by Wm. Theodore De Bary (1958). New York: Columbia University Press, pp. 31-32.
2. Siwan Anderson and Debraj Rey (2012). "The Age Distribution of Missing Women in India." *Economic and Political Weekly*, Vol. 47 (47-48), p. 82.
3. *Ibid.*, p. 87.
4. http://www.census2011.co.in/census/state/punjab.html. Retrieved 12 December 2012.
5. *Ibid.*
6. http://www.tribuneindia.com/2012/20120815/punjab.html. Retrieved 25 November 2012.
7. Shahid Perwez, Roger Jeffery, Patricia Jeffery (2012). "Declining Child Sex Ratio and Sex Selection in India: A Demographic Epiphany? *Economic and Political Weekly*, Vol. 47 (33), p. 73.

8. *Oh Naar Sulakhani, Jin Pehlan Jammi Laxmi.*
9. http://www.nytimes.com/2012/01/04/world/asia/04iht-letter.html. Retrieved 12 June 2012.
10. *Ibid.*
11. Punjab Election Watch 2012 (2012). Delhi: A Report by Association for Democratic Reform.
12. *Frontier*, September 30, 2012.
13. *Ibid.*
14. *Ibid.*
15. An Indian Machiavelli who lived in 4th century BC. His famous book the *Arthashastra (Statecraft) is a must read for government officials, military strategists, and politicians.*
16. An Indian proverb.
17. These promises were contained in the Congress Manifesto. See *The Tribune*, January 16, 2012.
18. *The Bhagavad Gita* (1962). Translated by Juan Mascaro. New York: Penguin, p. 58.
19. 'Jin Prem Kio Tin He Prabh Pio' in *Sri Dasam Granth Sahib* (1999), Delhi: South Asian Books, p. 30.
20. See Mao Ze Dong (1960). *On Contradiction.* Peking: Foreign Languages Press.
21. A promise from the Congress Manifest. See *The Tribune*, January 16, 2012.
22. This quote is attributed to Alex de Tocqueville, but its validity is in question.

9

M-for-Money and V-for-Victory

Statistics are like bikinis. What they reveal is suggestive,
but what they conceal is vital

— Anonymous quote

Money is called the mother's milk of electoral politics. In a strange fashion, this mother's milk has presented the biggest challenge to the health of democracy everywhere. The cost of fighting elections, from local to national levels, has increased the dependency of politicians on wealthy individuals in the population. In order to seek public office, the individuals must either be independently wealthy, or must have the ability to raise enormous sums. At one time in the history of European and North American democracies, the right to vote was limited only to wealthy males with substantial property[1]. In the era of universal suffrage, it seems, the right to contest elections has gone to wealthy males with substantial property. Every Indian election, for state assembly or national parliament, has witnessed the trend of two variables moving up: the cost of campaigns and the number of elected *Crorepatis*. In 2004, there were 156 *Crorepatis* in Lok Sabha, and in 2009, this number increased to 315[2]. Another noticeable trend points out that the value of assets of politicians has gone up from election to election. It is not known whether all these politicians are engaged in highly profitable business ventures, or if assets have a tendency to move up simply with electoral success. An Indian proverb says that 'the thief that is not caught is a king'. Unless proven otherwise, elected officials are honourable gentlemen. The dictionary of parliamentary language confirms this status.

There have been attempts to check the role of big money in Indian elections. One such attempt was made by Prime Minister Indra Gandhi in

1969. The Indian business community was prohibited from contributing to the campaigns of candidates and political parties. Meantime, through the license-permit-raj introduced with socialist rhetoric, she managed to initiate a new method of illegal funding with cash for favours dished out to favourite business houses. In other words, what was legal, open and transparent was made illegal, closed, and clandestine. The policy was reversed by her son, Prime Minister Rajiv Gandhi, in 1985 after winning a massive victory in parliamentary elections. Nothing changed in practice because most business houses were used for clandestine dealings with politicians and parties. Among the giants of Indian industry, only Tata industries have created a legal model of funding "which gives funds to all political parties on the basis of certain minimum vote share"[3]. Another attempt was made to reform the electoral system of India with the appointment of the Indrajit Gupta Committee on State Funding in 1998. Through their submissions, all major national parties of India defended the status quo in the electoral process and managed to put an end to any serious efforts to reform the system. As a result, the election process is still conducted under the 'Representation of the Peoples Act, 1951'.

Elections are conducted under the guidance and authority of the Election Commission of India. This constitutionally mandated body is independent of both the legislative and executive branches. On the initiative of the EC, all political parties agreed to draft a code of conduct. Despite this common agreement, all political parties have violated the code with impunity. The most successful effort of the EC to conduct free and fair elections has been the use of Electronic Voting Machines (EVM) in all elections. The old problem of stealing and stuffing the ballot boxes with muscle power disappeared with the introduction of EVMs. However, the problem of money power in elections has not only continued but increased. Just before the elections, the EC "instructed the candidates to open separate bank accounts for their election expenses and to make all election expenses through the said bank account"[4]. In order to check the distribution of cash to voters, the EC also banned carrying of cash over the amount of 2.5 *Lakh*. The law also required candidates to disclose all donations over ₹ 20,000. The spending limit for candidates contesting state assembly elections was set at ₹ 16 *Lakh*. In practice, however, there was no limit as candidates spent millions to win their seats. The Union Cabinet Minister and Congress Member of Parliament from Ludhiana, Minish Tiwari, noted that in one constituency in his electoral district[5], a candidate apparently spent "between ₹ 18 and 20 *Crore*"[6] .

In the last 48 hours of the campaign, the cash flowed like liquor in Punjab. A journalist noted that "cash-for-vote....appeared to have replaced door to door canvassing a few hours ahead of the voting to elect the next legislative assembly in Punjab"[7]. It was noted that in the area of Lambi, where Chief Minister Parkash Singh Badal faced his brother Gurdas Singh Badal, "each vote commanded about ₹ 1500." In Gidderbaha, where the Chief Minister's nephew and People's Party leader, Manpreet Singh Badal, was a candidate, the supporters of candidates "had been offering ₹ 1000 for each vote"[8]. The supporters of each candidate would contact a senior member of the family and ask him "to swear in the name of God at a religious place. The money would be handed to him only after he made the promise to fetch votes"[9]. The EC's notice of not carrying more than 2.5 *Lakh* in cash gave a legal excuse to Punjab police to harass ordinary citizens, while billions flowed from candidates to voters in broad day light. This practice of cash-for-vote, along with money paid to party leaderships to secure a nomination, has forced candidates to spend '18 to 20 Crores', if not more, to win or lose assembly seats.

In Dholpur, both the Akali candidate, Jagir Singh, and the Congress candidate, Amar Singh, were working feverishly with their teams to move cash directly to voters and power blocs of the constituency. Jagir Singh asked his grandson to phone all those who had promised but did not deliver the cash. He knew that 'the money you dream about will not pay your bills'[10]. Less money was received from traders and businessmen of the area than in the last election. It worried Jagir Singh not because he had a dearth of funds but because it perhaps indicated that the business community had expected the Congress to win. The money from supporters and well-wishers came in small amounts, enough to pay for some day-to-day activities. Major funds were always provided by the business community, and by civil and police officers, NRIs and, of course, the mother's milk from the criminal underworld. Jagir Singh had a great respect for the latter, as the money they promised was delivered in full and on time. In anticipation of the Congress victory, some civil and police officers had started making excuses toward the end of the Akali-BJP government's term. The NRI fund also did not match their verbal commitments. A surprising source of funds arrived from a high ranking police officer stationed in a neighbouring state. This officer's home village was located in the Dholpur constituency, but the Indian Police Service had designated him cadre of the neighbouring state. He was in charge of the counter-insurgency operations, and thus accumulated enormous amount of money which came in the form of slush funds. Now, he was looking for an assignment in his home state. Among the candidates, he decided to fund both the Akali and the Congress candidates of this constituency. Election expenses had increased since the last election, and so did the personal wealth of Jagir Singh. In the absence of any outside funds, the Akali candidate was able to spend as much as he needed from his own pockets. Still political wisdom demanded that election funds must be raised from others. It's no wonder that 'the hands of a politician are always in someone else's pocket'.

Jagir Singh learned through his ground workers that based on reports from neighbouring constituencies, people were now expecting ₹ 1,000 per vote compared with the rate of ₹ 500 during the last election. Inflation was perhaps on everyone's mind. A recent survey of electors on the most important issues facing Punjab had indicated that price rise was considered the number one issue by an overwhelming 41 per cent of those surveyed followed by the issue of unemployment indicated by 22 per cent[11]. The issues of corruption and drug addiction were only on the mind of 9 and 7 per cent of the respondents respectively[12]. On financial and logistical grounds, no candidate likes this cash-for-vote business, but the ground realities of politics dictated that this necessary evil cannot be wished away. The poor families who were leaning toward the Akali candidate had been identified by his team. Their support, however, depended on the delivery of cash in advance. 'Poverty,' according to an Indian proverb, 'destroys all virtues'. The disease of cash-for-vote has spread to almost all groups of society, but it has become cancerous among the poor segments. In comparative terms, however, the real money was made by the people who were in charge of delivery. Jagir Singh had handed this responsibility to family members and trustworthy supporters, but the scope of the operation demanded the involvement of a large number of individuals. Many such individuals kept large amounts of cash from this delivery fund. In the states of Goa and Tamil Nadu, it has been observed, that newspaper vendors have also been recruited to deliver cash to homes with the morning delivery of newspapers[13]. In a remarkable fashion, this method completes one cycle of election-related briberies. The newspaper owners receive money for 'package deals', the journalists are paid to write favourable stories, the vendors get commission for delivering of cash, and the readers get paid to vote.

The Akali candidate had just dispatched the first platoon of Santa Clauses to deliver money when his grandson, Ajay, received a phone call from a *Dera* trustee of *Baba-Jee*. The message was short and simple:

please deliver the promised sum. The *Dera* had demanded 5 *Crores* to build homes for their disciples. It also claimed that *Baba-Jee* had 15,000 to 20,000 votes in the Dholpur constituency. Jagir Singh knew that the numbers did not exceed 5000 at most, and that the money demand was higher than the market rate. A deal, however, was reached with the diplomacy of a retired senior civil officer for 2 *Crores*. Although this rate was four times higher than the market rate, Jagir Singh agreed to pay the price as the *Dera* vote delivery to his candidacy was guaranteed. Moreover, Bhima's man had promised to carry any cost of the *Dera* deal. Jagir Singh remembered the days when *Dera* chiefs used to contribute to candidate and party funds in cash. As the secular electoral politics has degenerated, religious chiefs have assumed a higher status. Jagir Singh instructed Ajay to contact Bhima's man to deliver the funds to *Dera*. "Tell him it's urgent," said Jagir Singh. "I will visit *Baba-Jee* once the money is delivered."

On the other side, Amar Singh was trying to reach a final deal with another *Dera*. The *Dera* had a much larger base of followers, but in this constituency the number of disciples was not higher than the *Dera* of *Baba* Ahluwalia. Amar Singh was dealing with an area leader of the *Dera* who had demanded 3 Crores for sending a message to the followers. "*Baba-jee* and the *Dera* will not issue edicts to disciples, but a message will reach them through local congregations," said the local leader. Amar Singh wanted a better guarantee with a religious order. He knew that the *Dera* was known for its pro-Congress leanings, but that the followers may have independent minds. The Congress candidate was looking for some direct or indirect hints from the *Dera* chief to his followers. Amar Singh knew that if you 'pull someone by the ears, his head will follow'[14]. The local leader, however, made it abundantly clear that *Baba-Jee* would not be involved. At the same time, he assured him that the votes would be delivered and only to the Congress candidate. He recited a Punjabi proverb to help Amar Singh make a decision: 'You want to eat mangoes or count mango trees'. The real issue was votes, and this support would neutralize the impact of the other *Dera*'s support to the Akali candidate. Amar Singh decided to reach a final deal with a new deal of only 1 *Crore*, 50 *Lakh*.

The next challenge for Amar Singh was the issue of buying loans. The established practice was to pay banks, co-operative credit unions, and private lenders the amount owed by individuals and families in exchange for their votes. Amar Singh had mobilized a special team to verify if this practice of clearing loans was better than cash delivery to these families. In terms of logistics, the practice of loan payments was much more convenient. His team had split opinions on this issue after field investigation. In most families, the team discovered that women were in favour of clearing loans, but that men were more interested in cash. Men knew that the days of free liquor and drugs would end at the dusk of election-day. The cash in hands would ensure such supply in the next few weeks. The women knew their men very well and argued in favour of paying off their debts because cash in the hands of these men would disappear in no time. It was difficult to ascertain which method would ensure the votes of the entire family. Some in the team argued that women of the family should be taken in confidence, and that paying directly to their creditors was the best course of action. The majority, however, argued in favour of cash because most members believed that men were the decision makers in their families. In this patriarchal society, a man with an IQ level of an Arctic temperature thinks that he was created to make decisions for the rest of the family. Needless to say, Amar Singh and his team opted for cash delivery.

In the meantime, the campaign team brought two more demands on the liquor front. The first was the fear of many drunkards that liquor would disappear from their homes after election-day. They were looking for some transition period stock. The second demand came from prominent people who argued that the campaign workers were dumping cheap alcohol at their homes. They demanded higher quality whisky for consumption and distribution in their networks. The campaign workers had forgotten an Indian saying that 'the poor man looks for food, the rich man for appetite'. Amar Singh immediately ordered the delivery of one case of local distillery whisky per household for the former, and two cases of premier whisky per household for the latter. The last moments of the campaign were psychologically more challenging for each candidate. At a time when Amar Singh was knee deep in handling various demands, the PPP candidate's friend arrived to make a deal. Hungary for votes, Amar Singh thought the envoy had brought him some political news. Garg was a banker and the news related to his banks. Based on data from their branches in the Dholpur constituency, the Garg financial team had made a list of some 3,000 families with debts ranging from ₹ 7000 to 10000. On average, each family owed 8500 Rupees. "Since Garg knows he has no chance of winning," said the envoy, "he is willing to give this list to you. Instead of 8500, you can just pay 4500 per family and the banks will clear all these debts." Amar Singh had heard through the grapevine that the first offer of this debt was made to Jagir Singh, which he refused. Secondly, it was rumoured that most of these debts were simply dead loans. The debtors simply had no desire to pay back these loans. Thirdly, the team had already decided to go for all cash. Amar Singh politely refused the envoy's offer, and requested his political support as he was departing.

The trade union leader, Comrade Kulwant Singh, brought some good news for Amar Singh. More than two dozen key supporters of the BSP candidate were willing to bring their votes to the Congress leader. "Although they may exaggerate, I think each of these men can deliver from 20 to 40 votes," said Kulwant. "They were demanding money based on their inflated egos, but finally settled for 60,000 to 100,000". Amar Singh knew that the costs of the campaign were rising with every ticking second, but he also did not want to take a chance. He knew that Kulwant had an influence on Dalits and he would ensure the delivery of votes. As Amar Singh gave him a green signal, Kulwant came up with another exciting idea. "We should think about giving around ₹ 10,000 each to *Pandits* (Hindu Priests) and *Pathis* (Sikh Priests) of large *Mandirs* and *Gurdwaras* in the area. For smaller temples, we can offer a smaller amount. These people exercise traditional religious authority over the masses. But we should exclude the *Gurdwaras* controlled by the SGPC because their *Pathis* are indirect employees of the Akali Dal and they are afraid of Akali politicians," said Kulwant, as he looked at Amar Singh's glowing face. "Even if they don't have huge congregations," continued Kulwant, "these *Shaitans* (devils) always have a few women in their circles"[15]. Amar Singh laughed at the last statement in agreement, and thought Kulwant was hitting the nail on the head.

Comrade Kulwant Singh was on a roll as he changed the subject. "I've noticed a number of NRIs in your campaign," said the union leader. "My opinion is that you should take their money but not rely on their votes. Most of them have disputes with their family members and relatives over property and assets. Thus, they have no influence over any votes. They run around in their fancy clothes and cars to show off their Canadian and American passports. A police officer told me that many of these big name wealthy NRIs are criminals". The Congress candidate knew that Kulwant was telling the truth, but Amar Singh had a lot of support among NRI criminals. Their election fund was higher than in 2007. Many NRIs were expecting a Congress victory because history showed that no incumbent government had ever been re-elected in Punjab. Amar Singh knew that a large number of former terrorists and criminals had settled abroad. Many have pending criminal cases in the courts of Punjab. In their absence, thousands of NRIs have been declared 'proclaimed offenders' by the judiciary. Legally they face immediate jail upon return. In practice, however, most roam free with the help of powerful politicians like Amar Singh Kulwant noticed that Amar Singh was silent on the issue of NRIs, so he decided to change the subject and cheer him up. "The election is going in your favour in Dholpur, and there is no doubt the Congress is headed for a victory in the state," said Kulwant. "Our party insiders in the state leadership think you will get a major cabinet portfolio." With these cheerful words, the Comrade said good-bye to Amar Singh.

For a moment, Amar Singh started pondering over the chance of victory for him and the Congress party. The opinion polls had already gone in the favour of his party with each one predicting a majority government for the Congress. While a Star News poll had predicted a 63 seat majority, the India Today poll gave 69 seats to the Congress in a 117 seat assembly[16]. The same India Today poll had predicted a 27 seat loss for the Akali-BJP coalition[17]. Opinion polls reveal some interesting stuff, but they also conceal something vital. The art of political polling requires massive amounts of data relating to politics, from the electoral lists to the identification of well-known cleavages in society, such as caste, religion, region, language, gender, age, urban versus rural etc. In a random sample, the pollster will work with a mathematical model for probability so that each person in the data has an equal chance of being selected. Even with the rigorous application of polling methodology, it faces several challenges in trying to predict political opinions with certainty. At best, the poll captures the opinion of a subject at a given moment. One of the biggest challenges in Punjab is the unwillingness of people to share their partisan opinions in public. In rural areas, the politics of political vendetta has been rampant during both the Akali-BJP and the Congress regimes. During the current Akali-BJP administration, the Congress claimed that more than 50,000 false police cases were registered against its cadre[18]. The Congress manifesto declared that these cases would be investigated and that guilty officials would be punished.

Regardless of the opinion polls, the day of the real polls arrived with patches of fog in the early morning hours. The armies of political workers from both major candidates were ready to take their supporters to the polling booths. Unlike in previous elections, however, the EC did not allow any political party to camp near the polling booths. Thus, *Chaa* and *Pakoras* had to be served from supporters' homes. The sovereigns of the land were standing in long lines even before the polling stations opened. The right to vote with a secret ballot gave the citizens of the Republic a unique and powerful tool to select its rulers. Both candidates were busy in pushing their teams to get the vote out. The teams had standing orders to ensure the full supply of drugs, liquor and money on demand. In the game of politics, there are no runner-ups. Winning is everything. Tit for tat strategy was adopted by both sides with the deployment of muscle brigades from the criminal underworld. Media people were standing ready around 'sensitive booths'[19]. Journalists were not happy as there were only some minor skirmishes to report. The employees of polling firms were annoyed at many people for not revealing the party and the candidate they had voted for[20]. Despite this problem, it did not stop the polling firms to start analyzing the data from exit polls immediately after the polls closed. The publication of such polls, however, was not allowed by the Election Commission because campaigns were still going on in other states, most importantly the largest electoral battle in the state of Uttar Pradesh (UP).

The election ended on the evening of January 30, 2012, but the results could not be declared until March 6, after the polling ended in UP. The Election Commission was of the view that all four states' results must come at the same time. For candidates, it was mental torture of monumental proportions. The period of 35 days between the end of the election and the declaration of results felt like a century. For ordinary people, life during this period was smoother because there was no government, and the officialdom was still operating under the orders of the Election Commission. The political workers wasted their time by engaging in heated claims of victory for their candidates and the parties. The bookies were busy in taking orders, and by all accounts the Congress victory was the most certain winner in the domain of gambling. Jagir Singh and Amar Singh started making rounds of *Mandirs* and *Gurdwaras* to offer prayers to Gods. The foundations of both Hinduism and Sikhism are based on the philosophical principle of truth. *Satyameva Jayate* (truth alone triumphs) is the clarion call of Hindu philosophy. The Sikh holy book begins with the words—*ad sach* (truth in the beginning), *jugad sach* (truth throughout the ages), *hai bhee sach* (truth in the present), Nanak *hosi bhee sach* (truth shall prevail, Oh Nanak)[21]. How exactly the *Pandits* and *Pathi*s reconcile the contradictions between the philosophical tenets of religion and the lives of habitual liars in offering prayers for their success is a puzzle for gods, but it's secular interpretation is simple that money and power prevails.

The struggle for power saw a ray of hope as the UP polls closed on March 3, and the polling agencies started releasing statistics. All major exit polls for Punjab, with the exception of the Indian Broadcasting Network, predicted a Congress victory in a range of 62 to 68 seats[22]. Pleased by the

IBN exit polls' favourable position, the Akali Dal countered the claims of other polls by suggesting that higher polling in this election indicated an Akali victory, as has been the case in the past. The voter turn-out rate of 78.6 per cent was indeed 3 per cent higher than in 2007[23]. A more positive indicator for the Akalis was a much higher polling of 81 per cent in rural areas, where the Akali Dal had most of its support base, compared with only 69 per cent in urban areas and 78.6 per cent in semi-urban areas. Moreover, the polling of 81.2 per cent among Sikh voters, the base of the Akali Dal, compared with 74.4 per cent among Hindus, boosted the morale of Akali politicians. As the Congress, the BSP, and left parties generally do better among *Dalits*, the polling among this segment was slightly lower with 78 per cent compared with 78.8 per cent among the non-*Dalit* voters[24]. Both sides were highlighting statistics that favoured them, but the truth was still lying hidden in the computer data base of Voting Machines guarded by paramilitary forces. The air of confidence in the Congress camp was shared by the majority the chattering class. Civil and Police officers started making subterranean visits to the Congress Chief's house. Both sides, however, had secret spies watching the visits of these officers to Chief Ministerial candidates, Parkash Singh Badal and Amarinder Singh. Along with officers, the candidates were keen to be seen by their respective party leaders to secure cabinet positions. Yet no one was sure of victory, and thus the astrologers of Punjab had a busy season.

On March 6, the biggest outdoor media stage was organised by the Congress Party in Chandigarh. The elusive party chief, Capt. Amarinder Singh, was going to address the media in open after the assured victory by most opinion and exit polls. The Congress leaders and candidates, including Amar Singh, had prepared their statements to thank party leaders Rahul and Sonia Gandhi. The results, however, shocked almost everyone in the rank and file of the Congress party. As the results poured in quickly from voting machines, the Congress tent started deserting faster than the speed of light. Captain Amarinder Singh refused to show his face in public. The results of the real poll contradicted the predictions of many *Pandits* and pollsters.

In a multi-party contest, the Akali Dal won 56 seats with 2 per cent less of the popular vote and 8 seats more than in 2007. Its alliance partner, the Bhartya Janata Party, won 12 seats with 1 per cent less of the popular vote and 7 seats less than in 2007. The Congress vote share was down less than 1 per cent from 40.90 in 2007 to 40.09 per cent in 2012, but it won 2 more seats than in previous election for a total of 46 seats. Manpreet Badal led *Sanjha Morcha* (the united front) won 6.14 per cent of the popular vote but failed to open an account in the Punjab Legislature with any seats. The Bahujan Samaj Party's vote share stayed almost the same at 4.29 per cent, and, just like in the previous election, the party failed to win a single seat. Two Akali rebels and one Congress rebel won as independents. Apart from this 'unexpected' Akali victory, some interesting facts have been revealed by statistics about the social basis of voting. In terms of gender, the Congress vote bank among both men and women remained unchanged since the last election of 2007. For the Akali-BJP coalition, the percentage of men's votes declined from 44 per cent in 2007 to 40 per cent in 2012. Among women voters, the coalition also lost 4 per cent as the percentage declined from 48 per cent in 2007 to 44 in 2012. While the vote share of the saffron coalition among voters with less than a high school education did not witness much change, the biggest drop was among college graduates going from 50 per cent in 2007 to 42 per cent in 2012. The Congress share of votes among all levels of educated and non-educated voters did not fluctuate in any major fashion. The rural-urban cleavage showed that for both the Akali-BJP and the Congress, the rural vote base remained unchanged. Among the urban voters, while the Congress did not see any change in its support base, the Akali-BJP support declined from 46 per cent in 2007 to 36 per cent in 2012. In terms of caste, the biggest loss for the Congress was recorded among Hindu *Dalits* and Hindu backward castes. Its vote share among Hindu *Dalits* went from 53 per cent in 2007 down to 37 per cent in 2012, and among Hindu backward castes, the decline was from 51 per cent to 37 per cent. The Congress, however, recorded no real loss among Sikh *Dalits* and Sikh backward castes. On the other hand, the Akali-BJP combination increased its support base among both Hindu and Sikh *Dalits* and backward castes. Its support among Hindu *Dalits* increased from 29 per cent in 2007 to 33 per cent in 2012, and among Hindu backward castes it went from 36 in 2007 to 40 per cent in 2012. Similarly, among Sikh *Dalits* the Akali-BJP coalition increased its support from 30 per cent in 2007 to 34 per cent in 2012. Among the Sikh backward castes, the coalition support increased from 42 per cent in 2007 to 46 per cent in 2012. Interestingly, the Akali Dal and the BJP are known for their support base among upper caste Sikhs and upper caste Hindus respectively, but their share of the vote declined among these segments of the population. While the Congress increased its share of votes among Hindu upper castes from 45 per cent in 2007 to 48 per cent in 2012, the Akali-BJP combination support declined from 43 per cent in 2007 to 34 per cent in 2012. Among upper caste *Jatt* Sikhs, the Congress support remained virtually the same at 31 per cent, and the Akali-BJP declined from 60 per cent in 2007 to 52 per cent in 2012[25].

The results brought huge celebrations at Jagir Singh's house as he won his own seat and his party was set to form the next government. Amar Singh, on the other hand, was receiving medical treatment after his personal and party defeat. In the Dholpur constituency of 151,000 registered voters, more than 118,000 votes were polled. The results indicated a close contest between the Akali Dal's Jagir Singh winning with 53,151 compared with the Congress candidate Amar Singh's 51,379. The PPP candidate Garg received merely 963 votes but the rebel Congress candidate got 4,179 votes. 'When brothers fight to the death, a stranger inherits their father's estate'[26]. Amar Singh was quick to blame his defeat on this Congress rebel and cursed party leadership for allowing this man to play into the hands of the opposition. A lesser man takes credit for a success and blames others for a failure. A great man, however, assumes responsibility for a failure and credits others for a success. There was no time for philosophy for defeated Congress candidates as the blame game started. While most of them blamed state party chief, Amarinder Singh, the party's national president, Sonia Gandhi, blamed the "weak choice of candidates and weak organisational structure" of the party[27]. The Congress also blamed the PPP for playing the spoiler. According to Sonia Gandhi, "the PPP damaged us in 23 seats."[28] The above data from elections shows that the Akali-BJP coalition lost most of their base among upper caste *Jatt* Sikhs, Hindu upper castes, and the college educated strata. While the Congress retained its base among these segments, its losses were heavy among Hindu *Dalits* and backward castes. The PPP seems to have gained most of its support from *Jatt* Sikhs and the college educated segment. Sonia Gandhi's blame game was based on an assumption that in the absence of the PPP, the votes that shifted away from the Akali-BJP's traditional base would have moved to the Congress. It was also noticeable that the Akali-BJP gains were mostly among the traditional Congress vote bank of *Dalits* and other poor segments. This was surely a benefit they had gained from *Atta-Daal* and other pro-poor schemes implemented during the last 5 years.

For statistics lovers, a history was made by the Akali-BJP with back to back victories in Punjab. Otherwise, it was business as usual. Dynastic politics had received another stamp of democratic legitimacy. The grip of *Crorepatis* on electoral politics became stronger with their numbers increasing from 77 in 2007 to 101 in 2012[29]. In the last assembly, the average wealth of each *Crorepati* MLA was 5.73 *Crores* which had now increased to 9.17 *Crores*. The Congress MLA, Kewal Singh Dhillon, recorded the highest growth from 6.83 *Crores* in 2007 to 78.51 in

2012. The assets of the Akali Chief, Sukhbir Singh Badal, went from 67.98 *Crores* in 2007 to 90.86 *Crores* in 2012[30]. While most candidates received the help of the criminal underworld, the number of MLAs with criminal backgrounds only increased by one (from 21 in 2007 to 22 in 2012)[31]. It was observed that candidates had won, or lost, their seats with multi-*Crore* budgets, not a single elected MLA reported an expense of the legally permissible limit of 16 *Lakh*. On average, each MLA reported a spending of ₹ 677,887, which is 42 per cent of the permissible limit[32]. Thus, each Member of the Legislative Assembly of Punjab began his or her new term as a law-maker with a lie on the sworn affidavit. A new government was formed through a democratic process to rule with dictatorial powers for the next 5 years. It has become a cliché to say that the real test of a democracy is measured by how it treats minority opinion. A majority mandate does not and should not mean that any alternative and opposite viewpoint has no place in the governance. The essence of democracy is captured in the legislative chambers only when all pros and cons of various temporary and permanent issues are discussed and debated from every possible vantage point. According to an old Indian proverb, 'it is better to be blind than to see things from one point of view'. In Punjab politics, however, the difference between the governing party and the opposition on most issues is nothing more than Tweedledum versus Tweedledee. Although they hardly differ on policy matters, the intolerance shown by the ruling parties to any slight variation of opinion from their own has presented a challenge to the spirit of democratic debate. Another emerging trend toward authoritarianism in Punjab is the way in which state's civil and police bureaucracy is used as the personal fiefdom of the ruling party. In a highly charged partisan environment, the officers of civil and police forces are identified with parties, instead of as a non-partisan professional force. The lack of practical checks and balances in the system has endangered the freedoms and liberties enshrined in the constitution. Thus, in the state of diminishing opposition to hold the rulers accountable, a situation has developed that echoes a warning from the Roman satirist Juvenal: "But who will guard the Guardians themselves?"[33]

References

1. The same rule applied to electoral lists during the British raj.
2. The figures are based on affidavits submitted by Members of Parliament. These statistics hide two important variables: deliberate understatement of

the real value of assets, and transfer of assets to the names of family members and even relatives of politicians. These figures are taken from *The Hindu*, March 1, 2012.

3. Samya Chatterjee and Niranjan Sahoo (2012), Eds. "Campaign Finance Reforms in India: Issues and Challenges", New Delhi: Observer Research Foundation, p. 4.

4. See the guidelines at http://eci.nic.in.

5. There are 13 parliamentary electoral districts in Punjab, and each of these districts contains 9 MLA constituencies within its boundaries.

6. Samya Chatterjee and Niranjan Sahoo (2012), Eds., op. cit., p. 4.

7. *India Today*, January 30, 2012.

8. *Ibid.*

9. *Ibid.*

10. An Indian proverb.

11. "Fourteenth Assembly Elections in Punjab" (2012). *Economic and Political Weekly*, Vol. 47 (14), p. 75.

12. *Ibid.*

13. Samya Chatterjee and Niranjan Sahoo (2012), Eds., op. cit., p. 4.

14. An Indian proverb.

15. In *Persian Letters*, French enlightenment philosopher Montesquieu writes: "That," he replied, "is a preacher, and, what is worse, a spiritual adviser. As such, he knows more than husbands do. He knows a woman's weak point; and they know what his is too." New York: Penguin Publisher, 1973, p. 105.

16. *India Today*, January 19, 2012.

17. *Ibid.*

18. *The Tribune*, January 16, 2012.

19. This term is used by the Election Commission to identify polling booths with the imminent danger of violence. As a result, extra security is arranged to keep peace around those polling stations.

20. The surveys done by some research institutes during and after the Election Day solicited a more positive response. I met some graduate students from Guru Nanak Dev University conducting surveys on the ground. They would go to pre-selected households and sit with the people in their homes. The team members introduced themselves to individuals and families and explained the nature and purpose of the surveys." After having tea and some conversation, the individuals opened up to us with all the information we needed," said a young surveyor from the political science department of GNDU.

21. The words are from Japaji Sahib composed by the first Guru, Nanak, in the Adi Granth.
22. *Times of India*, March 3, 2012.
23. "Fourteenth Assembly Elections in Punjab" (2012), op. cit., p. 71.
24. All this poll data is taken from *Ibid.*, p. 72.
25. All data from table 3a of *Economic and Political Weekly*'s special statistics report on "Fourteenth Assembly Elections in Punjab" (2012), op. cit., p. 73.
26. An Ibo proverb.
27. www.mid-day.com/news/2012/mar.080312-sonia-blames-party-weakness-for-debacle.htm. Retrieved 11 January 2013.
28. *Ibid.*
29. My personal observation is that all MLAs in the Punjab Assembly are Crorepatis. The statistics of 101 are based on affidavits submitted by candidates related to their personal wealth and assets. The figures in affidavits are understated. Candidates shift properties and assets to the names of other family members, and the value of properties and other assets is grossly underestimated.
30. All data on the candidates assets is taken from *The Tribune*, March 12, 2012.
31. "Analysis of Criminal and Financial Details of Newly Elected MLAs for Punjab" (2012). New Delhi: Association for Democratic Reform, p. 5.
32. *The Tribune*, April 18, 2012.
33. Cited in Leslie Lipson (1965). *The Great Issues of Politics: An Introduction to Political Science.* Englewood Cliffs, New Jersey: Prentice-Hall, p. 73.

Bibliography

Ahluwalia, Jasbir Singh (1983). *The Sovereignty of the Sikhs Doctrine*. New Delhi: Bahri Publications.

Ailes, Roger (1988), *You are the Message: Secrets of the Master Communicators*. Homewood, IL: Dow Jones Irwin.

"Analysis of Criminal and Financial Details of Newly Elected MLAs for Punjab." (2012). New Delhi: Association for Democratic Reforms (ADR).

Anand, Jagjit Singh (1991). *Punjab Problem: Facets*. New Delhi: Kay Kay Printers.

Ananda, Parkash (1996). *History of the Tribune*. Chandigarh: Tribune Trust.

"Anandpur Sahib Resolution (1973)", in Abida Samiuddin, ed. (1985). *The Punjab Crisis: Challenge and Response*. Delhi: Mittal Publications.

Arora, Dolly (1995). "On the Tragedy of Public Domain: Corruption, Victimization and the New Policy Regime." *Indian Journal of Public Administration*, Vol. 41 (3): 383-394.

Asher, Herbert (1988). *Polling and the Public: What Every Citizen Should Know*. Washington, D.C.: Congressional Quarterly Press.

Ashraf, Tariq (2004). *Election 2004: A Profile of Indian Parliamentary Elections since 1952*. New Delhi: Bookwell Publishing.

Azad, Nirmal Singh (1987). "Distorted Economic Development: Affluence and Backwardness in Punjab", in Gopal Singh, ed. *Punjab Today*. Delhi: Intellectual Publishing House.

Bakshi, S.R., Sita Ram Sharma and S. Gujrani (2008). *Contemporary Political Leadership of India: Parkash Singh Badal*. Delhi: APH Publishing.

Bal, Gurpreet and Parmjit Judge (2012). "Innovations, Entrepreneurship and Development: A Study of the Scheduled Castes in Punjab". *Journal of*

Entrepreneurship, Vol. 19 (1): 43-52.

Banerjee, Anil Chandra (1983). *The Sikh Gurus and the Sikh Religion.* New Delhi: Munshiram Manoharlal.

Banerjee, Sumanta (1984). "Punjab: The Best Lack all Conviction, While the Worst are Full of Passionate Intensity." *Economic and Political Weekly*, Vol. 19 (27): 1019-1021.

Banga, Indu (1988), "The Crisis of Sikh Politics (1940-1990)", in Joseph T. O'Connell, et al, eds. *Sikh History and Religion in Twentieth Century.* Toronto: University of Toronto Press.

Bhan, Susheela, ed. (1995). *Criminalization of Politics.* New Delhi: Shipra.

"Black Laws in Punjab: Report of an Enquiry." (1985), *Economic and Political Weekly*, Vol. 20 (19): 826-830.

Brar, K.S (1993). *Operation Bluestar: The True Story.* New Delhi: UBS Publishing.

Brass, Paul (1973). *Language, Religion and Politics in North India.* Cambridge: Cambridge University Press.

Chatterjee, Samya and Niranjan Sahoo (2012). "Campaign Finance Reforms in India: Issues and Challenges." New Delhi: Observer Research Foundation.

Chand, Attar (1989). *Jawaharlal Nehru and Politic in Punjab.* New Delhi: HK Publishers.

Chopra, Kanchan (1984). "Distribution of Agricultural Assets in Punjab: Some Aspects of Inequality." *Economic and Political Weekly*, Vol. 27 (49&50): 29-38.

Cicero, Quintus Tullius (2012). *How to Win an Election: An Ancient Guide for Modern Politician.* Translated by Philip Freeman, Princeton, NJ: Princeton University Press.

Chima, J.S. (2010). *The Sikh Separatist Insurgency in India: Political Landscape and Ethnonationalist Movement.* New Delhi: Sage Publications.

Clarke, Thurston (2008). *The Last Campaign: Robert F. Kennedy and 82 Days that Inspired America.* New York: Henry, Halt and Company.

Clayton, D.M. (2010). *The Presidential Election of Barack Obama: A Critical Analysis of a Racially Transcendent Strategy.* New York: Routledge.

The Code of Sikh Conduct and Conventions (1994). Amritsar: Gurdwara Prabandhik Committee.

Cohen, Stephen P. (1990). *The Indian Army: Its Contributions to the Development of a Nation.* Delhi: Oxford University Press.

Combs, James and Dan Nimmo (1993). *The New Propaganda: The Dictatorship of Palaver in Contemporary Politics.* New York: Longman Publishing.

Das, Pushpa (2012). "Drug Trafficking in India: A Case of Border Security." Occasional Paper Number 24, Delhi: Institute for Defense Studies and Analysis.

De Bary, Theodore, ed. (1958). *Sources of Indian Tradition.* Two Volumes, New York: Columbia University Press.

Deora, Man Singh (1991). *Akali Agitation to Operation Blue Star.* Two Volumes, Delhi: Anmol Publications.

Dragadze, Tamara (1996). "Self-Determination and the Politics of Exclusion." *Ethnic and Racial Studies*, Vol. 19 (2): 341-351.

Engineer, Asghar Ali (1991). "Lok Sabha Elections and Communalisation of Politics". *Economic and Political Weekly*, Vol. 26 (28): 1649-1652.

Fallows, James (1996). *Breaking the News: How the Media Undermine Democracy. New York: Pantheon Books.*

Faucheux, Ronald (2003). *Winning Elections: Political Campaign Management, Strategy, and Tactics.* Lanham, MD: M. Evans and Company.

"Fourteenth Assembly Elections in Punjab" (2012). *Economic and Political Weekly*, Vol. 47 (14): 71-75.

Fox, Richard (1984). *Lions of the Punjab: Culture in the Making.* Berkley: University of California Press.

Ghuman, Ranjit S. (2008). "Socio-Economic Crisis in Rural Punjab." *Economic and Political Weekly*, 43 (6): 12-16.

Girdner, Eddi and Kalim Saddiqui (1990). "The Political Economy of Communalism in India." *Asian Profile*, Vol. 18 (2): 147-162.

Grewal, J.S. (1996). *The Akalis: A Short History.* Chandigarh: Punjab Studies Publications.

_____ (1990). *The New Cambridge History of India: The Sikhs of Punjab.* Cambridge: Cambridge University Press.

Grewal, J.S. (1975). *From Guru Nanak to Maharaja Ranjit Singh: Essays in Sikh History.* Amritsar: Guru Nanak Dev University.

Guha, Ramachandra (2011). *Makers of Modern India.* Cambridge, Mas: Harvard University Press.

Gulati, Kailash Chander (1974). *The Akalis: Past and Present.* New Delhi: Ashajanak.

Gupta, Hari Ram (1984). *History of the Sikhs*. New Delhi: Munshiram Manoharlal Publishers.

Hansen, Thomas (1996). "Globalisation and Nationalist Imaginations: Hindutva's Promise of Equality Through Difference." *Economic and Political Weekly,* Vol. 31 (10): 603-616.

Herbest, Susan (1993). *Numbered Voices: How Opinion Polling Has Shaped American Politics.* Chicago: University of Chicago Press.

Ibbetson, Denzil (1987). *Punjab Castes: Races, Castes and the Tribes of the Punjab.* New Delhi.

Inder, Dev (2004). *Manual of Election Law in India.* New Delhi: Universal Law Publishing.

Jeffrey, Robin (1997). "Punjabi: The Sublimi Charge". *Economic and Political Weekly*, Vol. 32 (9): 1010-1015.

_____(1994). *What's Happening to India?: Punjab, Ethnic Conflict and the Test for Federation.* London: MacMillan.

Johal, S.S. (1989). *Future of Agriculture in Punjab.* Chandigarh: Center for Research in Rural and Industrial Development.

Josh, Bhagwan (1979). *Communist Movement in Punjab.* Delhi: Anupama Publications.

Kamnath, P.M. (1993). *Indian Politics Under Mrs. Gandhi: Reflective Essays* New Delhi: South Asian Publishers.

Kar, Dev (2011). "An Empirical Study on the Transfer of Black Money from India: 1948-2008." *Economic and Political Weekly*, Vol. 46 (15): 44-54.

Kaviraj, Sudipta (1986). "Indra Gandhi and Indian Politics." *Economic and Political Weekly*, Vol. 21 (38): 1697-1708.

Kaur, Jatinder (1989). *Punjab Crisis: The Political Perceptions of Rural Voters.* New Delhi: Ajanta Publications.

Kellner, Douglas (1995). *Television and the Crisis of Democracy.* Boulder, CO: Westview Press.

Kohli, Atul (1990). *Democracy and Discontent: India's Growing Crisis of Governability.* Cambridge: Cambridge University Press.

Kumar, Arun (2003). *Elections in India: Nehru to Vajpayee.* New Delhi: Gyan Publishing.

Kumar, B. Venkatesh (2009). *Electoral Reforms in India: Current Discourse.* New Delhi: Rawat Publications.

Kumar, Krishna (1990). "Hindu Revivalism and Education in North-Central India." *Social Scientist*, Vol. 18 (10): 4-26.

Kurtz, Howard (1998). *Spin Cycle: Inside the Clinton Propaganda Machine.* New York: The Free Press.

Latif, Syad Mohammed (1964). *History of the Punjab: From the Remotest Antiquity to the Present Time.* Delhi: Eurasia Publishers.

Limaye, Madhu (1992). *Decline of a Political System: Indian Politics at the Crossroads.* Allahabad: Wheeler Publishing.

Manor, James (1996). "Ethnicity and Politics in India". *International Affairs*, Vol. 72 (3): 459-475.

McLeod, W.H. (2001). *Exploring Sikhism: Aspects of Sikh Identity, Culture and Thought.* New Delhi: Oxford University Press.

_____ (1989). *The Sikhs: History, Religion and Society.* New York: Columbia University Press.

McMillan, Alistar (2006). *Standing at the Margins: Representation and Electoral Reservation in India.* New York: Oxford University Press.

Medvic, Stephen (2011). *New Directions in Elections and Campaigns.* New York: Routledge.

Mitra, Debkumar and Sudhir Dhar (2004). *The Mad, Mad World of Election.* New Delhi: Penguin Publishers.

Nayar, Baldev Raj (1966). *Minority Politics in the Punjab.* Princeton: Princeton University Press.

Nayar, Kamala (2004). *The Sikh Diaspora in Vancouver: Three Generations Amidst Tradition, Modernity and Multiculturalism.* Toronto: University of Toronto Press.

Nayar, Kuldip and Khushwant Singh (1984). *Tragedy of the Punjab: Operation Bluestar and After.* New Delhi: Vikas Publishers.

Oldenburg, Philip (2010). *India, Pakistan, and Democracy: Solving the Puzzle of Divergent Paths.* Abingdon: Routledge.

Omvedt, Gail (1990). "Twice-Born Riot Against Democracy." *Economic and Political Weekly*, Vol. 25 (39): 2195-2201.

Peters, Gretchen (2010). *Seeds of Terror: How Drugs, Thugs and Crime are Re-Shaping the Afghan War.* New York: MacMillan.

"Punjab Election Watch 2012" (2012). Delhi: A Report by Association for Democratic Reform (ADR).

Purewal, Shinder (2011). "Sikh Diaspora and the Movement for Khalistan." *Indian Journal of Political Science*, Vol. 72 (4): 1131-1142.

_____ (2001). "Religion, Violence and Security in South Asia." *Punjab Journal of Politics*, Vol. 33 (2): 3-21.

_____ (2000). "Quebec and Punjab: A Comparative Analysis of Two Autonomy Movements." *Proceedings of the Annual Conference of the British Columbia Political Studies Association*, Vancouver: Simon Fraser University.

_____ (2000). *Sikh Ethnonationalism and the Political Economy of Punjab.* New Delhi: Oxford University Press.

_____ (1999). "Agrarian Roots of Sikh Ethnonationalism." *Proceedings of the Annual Conference of the British Columbia Political Studies Association,* Vancouver: University of British Columbia.

Prewez, Shahid, Ragu Jeffery, Patricia Jeffery (2012). "Declining Child Sex Ratio and a Sex Selection in India: A Demographic Epiphany?" *Economic and Political Weekly*, Vol. 47 (38): 72-80.

Puri, Harish (1993). *Ghadar Movement: Ideology, Organisation and Strategy.* Second Edition, Amritsar: Guru Nanak Dev University.

Rao, Anupama (2008). *The Caste Question: Dalits and the Politics of Modern India.* Berkley: University of California Press.

Roy, M. (2002). *Electoral Politics in India: Election Process and Outcomes, Voting Behaviour and Current Trends.* New Delhi: Deep and Deep.

Seetal, S.S. (1981). *The Sikh Misls and the Punjab.* Ludhiana: Lahore Book Shop.

Seidman, Steven (2008). *Posters, Propaganda, and Persuasion in Election Campaigns, and Around the World and Through History.* New York: Peter Lang Publishing.

Shah, A.M. (2007). *The Grassroots of Democracy: Field Studies of Indian Elections.* New Delhi: Permanent Black.

Shukla, Ashish (2010). "Drug Trafficking in Pakistan: Threat to Regional Security." *Journal of Himalayan and Central Asian Studies*, 14 (3): 2-12.

"The Sikh Gurdwara Act, 1925", in Major A.E. Barstow (1928). *The Sikhs: Ethnology.* Delhi: BR Publishing.

Singer, Wendy (2006). *A Constituency Suitable for Ladies: And Other Social Histories of Indian Election.* New York: Oxford University Press.

Singh, Khushwant (1992). *My Bleeding Punjab.* Delhi: UBS Publishers.

Singh, Manjit (2012). "A Re-Election in Punjab and the Continuing Crisis."

Economic and Political Weekly, Vol. 47 (13): 21-25.

Surjeet, Harkishan Singh (1991). *Happenings in Punjab: A Democratic Solution.* New Delhi: National Book Center.

Talbot, Ian (1996). *Khizr Tiwana, the Punjab Unionist Party and the Partition of India.* Abingdon: Routledge.

Tatla, D.S. (1998). *The Sikh Diaspora: The Search for Statehood.* Abingdon: Routledge.

Tumbe, Chinmoy (2012). "EU-India Bilateral Remittance". Working Paper Number 360, Bangalore: Indian Institute of Management.

Tzu, Sun (2002). *The Art of War.* Translated by Lionel Giles. Mineola, NY: Dover Publications.

"Vohra Committee Report." (1995), *Indian Journal of Public Administration,* Vol. 41 (3): 640.

Wallace, Paul and Ramashray Ray, Eds. (2011). *India's 2009 Elections: Coalition Politics, Party Competition, and Congress Continuity.* New Delhi: Sage Publications.

____, Eds. (2008). *India's 1999 Elections and 20th Century Politics.* New Delhi: Sage Publications.

Wilkinson, Steven (2006). *Votes and Violence: Electoral Competition and Ethnic Riots in India.* Cambridge: Cambridge University Press.

"Who are the Guilty?: Causes and the Impact of the Delhi Riots." (1984). Report Prepared by People's Union for Democratic Rights and People's Union for Civil Liberties, *Economic and Political Weekly*, Vol. 19 (47): 1979-1985.

Index